In the Shadow of the Babe

For Vernon
Maybe they'll get baseball in Jamaica someday

In the Shadow of the Babe

Interviews with Baseball Players Who Played With or Against Babe Ruth

by Brent Kelley

McFarland & Company, Inc., Publishers
Jefferson, North Carolina, and London

Acknowledgments: The courtesy of the men interviewed herein is acknowledged. For the most part, they have reached points in their lives where they can call their own shots, yet each chose to speak with me and answer all the questions I had.

These interviews, in altered (or greatly altered) form, have appeared over the past few years in *Sports Collectors Digest*. Thanks to Tom Mortenson, editor, and Rick Hincs, associate editor, for accepting them. The Ty Cobb remembrance has appeared twice in slightly different form in *Baseball Cards* magazine. Former editor Kit Kiefer is the one responsible for its publication both times.

A book of baseball interviews without pictures of the interviewees is incomplete. The following supplied the photos for this work: The National Pastime (Harvey Brandwein), George Brace, Flea Clifton, Bill Rogell, Overton Tremper, Russ Scarritt, the Detroit Tigers (Connie Bell actually found them), and Elmer D. Kapp.

Silhouette illustration on front cover by Mike Schacht

British Library Cataloguing-in-Publication data are available

Library of Congress Cataloguing-in-Publication Data

Kelley, Brent P.
In the shadow of the babe : interviews with baseball players who played with or against Babe Ruth / by Brent Kelley.
p. cm.
Includes bibliographical references and index.
ISBN 0-7864-0068-4 (sewn softcover : 50# alk. paper)
1. Baseball players—United States—Interviews. 2. Baseball—United States—History. 3. Ruth, Babe, 1895–1948. I. Title.
GV865.A1K43 1995
796.357'092'2—dc20
[B] 95-8337
CIP

Manufactured in the United States of America

McFarland & Company, Inc., Publishers
Box 611, Jefferson, North Carolina 28640

CONTENTS

PREFACE

All of the men interviewed here played with or against Babe Ruth. The interviews are arranged in the order of these men's major league debuts; in other words, pretty much in the order in which they saw the Babe. Some were his friends, some were only his opponents; one was already on the major league scene when Babe arrived in 1914, some came along in the middle of his time in the majors, and some caught him only at the very end. But they all remember Babe.

The first interview is perhaps not an interview in the truest sense. To a 12-year-old boy, the chance to talk baseball with the great Ty Cobb was the ultimate interview. Hearing Cobb argue that he was the greatest ballplayer of all time is something that one does not forget.

The stories of the other players are no less interesting. They recount their careers in and out of the game, but they also tell stories about the Babe. Some are new, some are eyewitness accounts of much repeated legends. Ray Benge wanted to see if Babe could really hit a ball as hard as they said he could; Gus Suhr played against him in the Babe's last big performance; Buddy Hassett was treated to a "Catholic" breakfast by Babe; Ray Hayworth caught rookie Tommy Bridges's wicked curve as Babe fanned to end a game.

Babe Ruth was born 100 years ago. He did not invent baseball, but it is here today because of him.

INTRODUCTION

Babe Ruth: Baseball's Salvation 1914–1935

Babe Ruth may or may not have been the greatest player in baseball history—that does not matter—but he was the most famous. From the time he joined the Yankees in 1920 until he retired as an active player in 1935, Babe Ruth *was* baseball.

There were several reasons for this. First, of course, he was a marvelous player. He was also charismatic; the people loved him and he loved the people.

He played in the country's largest and most important city, New York, where he was Visible (with a capital "V"). He might have hit as many—maybe more—home runs in Detroit or Cincinnati but the effect would not have been the same. Ruth may have made baseball, but he had to have New York to do it. There were 16

Babe Ruth (courtesy National Pastime).

teams then but the teams were in only ten cities. The American League had three cities not in the National League, but the National League had only two not in the American League. Therefore, playing for the Yankees, Babe could be seen by the fans in all major league cities except Cincinnati and Pittsburgh, the two smallest major league markets.

And, yes, Babe *made* baseball. The game was hurting in the wake of the Black Sox scandal, but 1920, the year that the investigation was completed and Commissioner Kenesaw Mountain Landis's judgment was announced, was also the year Babe Ruth joined the Yankees. Even after three-quarters of a century, the deal that brought him over from the Red Sox remains the worst transaction ever made.

And after he retired as an active player, he was still *the* attraction. Hired by the Brooklyn Dodgers as their first base coach (he could never remember the signs), his chief function was to take pregame batting practice, play first base in exhibition games, and sign autographs. The fans still came out to see him three years after his last game.

Babe Ruth's shadow was large, both literally and figuratively. Major league baseball in the 1920s and 1930s featured some of the game's greatest players: Lou Gehrig, Eddie Collins, Walter Johnson, Pie Traynor, Jimmie Foxx, Lefty Grove, Rogers Hornsby—the list is long and impressive. But the man they paid to see was the Babe.

So if the fans preferred Babe Ruth to Jimmie Foxx, what about mere mortals such as Ray Benge or Gene Desautels? For over two decades there were baseball players and there was Babe Ruth. Whether it was the 1927 Yankees sweeping the Pirates in the World Series or a midseason game between the Cubs and the Phillies, Babe Ruth was the reason people were there, whether Babe was there or not.

In 1924, the late Fred Haney was an infielder for the Tigers. In a game against the Yankees, little Fred (5′6″) hit his first major league home run, a poke that just cleared the fence and one of only eight home runs he would hit in his seven-year career. When the inning was over and Fred was trotting out to his third base position, he passed Ruth as he headed to the Yankee dugout. "You may still be ahead, big boy," Fred said to him, "but I'm gainin' on you." The Babe said nothing.

As fate would have it, Ruth came to bat for the Yankees that inning. He blasted a towering drive deep into the right field stands. As he approached third base, head down in his home run trot, he did not even look at Haney but said, "How do we stand now, kid?"

How Haney stood, and how all of baseball stood, was in his shadow. Babe's shadow covered everyone in the game, with the possible exception of one man.

George Herman (Babe, the Bambino, the Sultan of Swat) Ruth

Born February 6, 1895, Baltimore, MD
Died August 16, 1948, New York, NY
Ht. 6′2″ Wt. 215 Batted and Threw Left

Year	Team	G	AB	R	H	2B	3B	HR	RBI	SB	BA	SA
1914	BosA	5	10	1	2	1	0	0	0	0	.200	.300
1915		42	92	16	29	10	1	4	21	0	.315	.576
1916		67	136	18	37	5	3	3	16	0	.272	.419
1917		52	123	14	40	6	3	2	12	0	.325	.472
1918		95	317	50	95	26	11	11*	66	6	.300	.555*
1919		130	432	103*	139	34	12	29*	114*	7	.322	.657*
1920	NYA	142	458	158*	172	36	9	54*	137*	14	.376	.847*
1921		152	540	177*	204	44	16	59*	171*	17	.378	.846*
1922		110	406	94	128	24	8	35	99	2	.315	.672*
1923		152	522	151*	205	45	13	41*	131*	17	.393	.764*
1924		153	529	143*	200	39	7	46*	121	9	.378*	.739*
1925		98	359	61	104	12	2	25	66	2	.290	.543
1926		152	495	139*	184	30	5	47*	145*	11	.372	.737*
1927		151	540	158*	192	29	8	60*	164	7	.356	.772*
1928		154*	536	163*	173	29	8	54*	142*	4	.323	.709*
1929		135	499	121	172	26	6	46*	154	5	.345	.697*
1930		145	518	150	186	28	9	49*	153	10	.359	.732
1931		145	534	149	199	31	3	46*	163	5	.373	.700*
1932		133	457	120	156	13	5	41	137	2	.341	.661
1933		137	459	97	138	21	3	34	103	4	.301	.582
1934		125	365	78	105	17	4	22	84	1	.288	.537
1935	BosN	28	72	13	13	0	0	6	12	0	.181	.431
22 years		2503	8399	2174	2873	506	136	714	2211	123	.342	.690

**Led League*

World Series

Year	Team	G	AB	R	H	2B	3B	HR	RBI	SB	BA	SA
1915	BosA	1	1	0	0	0	0	0	0	0	.000	.000
1916		1	5	0	0	0	0	0	1	0	.000	.000
1918		3	5	0	1	0	1	0	2	0	.200	.600
1921	NYA	6	16	3	5	0	0	1	4	2	.313	.500
1922		5	17	1	2	1	0	0	1	0	.118	.176
1923		6	19	8	7	1	1	3	3	0	.368	1.000
1926		7	20	6	6	0	0	4	5	1	.300	.900
1927		4	15	4	6	0	0	2	7	1	.400	.800
1928		4	16	9	10	3	0	3	4	0	.625	1.375
1932		4	15	6	5	0	0	2	6	0	.333	.733
10 years		41	129	37	42	5	2	15	33	4	.326	.744

PITCHING RECORD

Year	Team	G	IP	W	L	PCT	BB	SO	H	SHO	SV	ERA
1914	BosA	4	23	2	1	.667	7	3	21	0	0	3.91
1915		32	217.2	18	8	.692	85	112	166	1	0	2.44
1916		44	323.2	23	12	.657	118	170	230	9*	1	1.75*
1917		41	326.1	24	13	.649	108	128	244	6	2	2.01
1918		20	166.1	13	7	.650	49	40	125	1	0	2.22
1919		17	133.1	9	5	.643	58	30	148	0	1	2.97
1920	NYA	1	4	1	0	1.000	2	0	3	0	0	4.50
1921		2	9	2	0	1.000	9	2	14	0	0	9.00
1930		1	9	1	0	1.000	2	3	11	0	0	3.00
1933		1	9	1	0	1.000	3	0	12	0	0	5.00
10 years		163	1221.1	94	46	.671	441	488	974	17	4	2.28

**Led League*

World Series

Year	Team	G	IP	W	L	PCT	BB	SO	H	SHO	SV	ERA
1916	BosA	1	14	1	0	1.000	3	4	6	0	0	0.64
1918		2	17	2	0	1.000	7	4	13	1	0	1.06
2 years		3	31	3	0	1.000	10	8	19	1	0	0.87

TY COBB

In No One's Shadow

1905–1928

"Mother! Mother! Ty Cobb lives in Atherton! Call him—see if I can meet him!" I was 12 at the time.

When I was eight or nine, I discovered baseball cards and, because of them, baseball. Until that time I don't believe I knew the game existed, although I knew I enjoyed throwing a rubber ball with anyone who was

***Above:* Ty Cobb (courtesy Detroit Tigers).**

willing. It never occurred to me that a sport built around this wonderfully shaped object existed.

But in 1949 or 1950, my stepfather bought me two packs of Bowman baseball cards and a love affair began that has lasted over 40 years. Early on, baseball was a very frustrating lover. I collected cards, but there were always some missing (e.g., 42 Dick Littlefield cards, but no Virgil Trucks). And I played the game well enough, but not quite as well as I wanted to. In fact, it's just been the last few years that I have quit trying to play it. My sons now play and I was unable to attend their games if I continued to play. Also it became apparent that no contract offers were coming to me after I turned 40 anyway, so I hung up my cleats. I was playing a summer league intended for college players and was the oldest participant by over 20 years, so I guess it was time.

In those first two packs of cards were Johnny Groth and Pat Mullin. I don't recall who else. Groth and Mullin played for the Tigers and, since I now had two Tigers, Detroit became my favorite team. Nothing has altered that in the years since.

I had discovered baseball cards but I was still uncertain what the men depicted on these cardboard delights actually did. I do not know when or how I came to fully understand what was going on, but by the time I was ten I was aware of such thrilling facts of life as box scores, baseball bats, statistics, and life's most indispensable reading material, *The Sporting News*.

With the discovery of *TSN* came the realization that baseball had been around for a while. Until then, for all I knew the game had been invented the day those Bowmans were printed. But, by saving my allowance, I was able to send away for several of the great publications *TSN* produces. Within their pages, I learned that baseball was, indeed, not born in my lifetime and that there were histories—glorious histories—behind each team.

For instance, the Tigers had once had a great ballplayer who came from the state in which I lived. A great Tiger from my home state immediately ascended to the heights of favoritism, although it had been nearly 25 years since he had last played. At the time I lived in Georgia, near Atlanta, so the player in question should be easily identified.

When I was 11, we moved to the then small town of Los Altos, California, about 35 miles down the peninsula from San Francisco. There a group developed the first Little League the area had known and I eagerly joined the team. From then on, the only thing that distracted me from some level of baseball participation was the discovery of girls a few years later. Since we did not play night games, I found the latter pursuit could best be dealt with after the games were over.

One day in 1953 I was listening to a San Francisco Seals' game when the announcer (I think his name was Bob Fouts) mentioned that Ty Cobb—*Ty Cobb*—lived in Atherton. Atherton was only ten or so miles up the peninsula. The great Ty Cobb lived within ten miles of me! "Mother! Mother! Ty Cobb lives in Atherton! Call him—see if I can meet him!"

My mother was not nearly as impressed by this bit of knowledge as I was and somehow did not share my excitement at the prospect of meeting him. Having spent a good deal of her life in Georgia, she was acquainted with his reputation. She assured me that he was not a very nice man and would not welcome the request, much less the intrusion.

I was quick to point out that we would never know if he minded if we did not ask. She was not easily swayed. However, I was less easily deterred. After several weeks of my being totally obnoxious, Mother (more to shut me up than anything else, I believe) called him, explained my desires, and asked if it would be possible for her to bring me by his house.

"When can you be here?" was Cobb's reply.

Well, Mom explained, it was not possible for us to come that day. (I was standing by her saying, "Yes we can! Yes we can!") Cobb then suggested that we come around ten the next morning and gave us directions to his house.

I could not believe it. I told my friends around the neighborhood and, for reasons that I do not understand to this day, most were not too impressed. One even told me that Ty Cobb was dead but, fortunately, one kid appreciated what I was about to do: "Geez, lucky guy!" That night I was so excited I had a very hard time falling to sleep.

We left the house around 9:30 and arrived at the Cobb house a few minutes before ten. Mr. Cobb greeted us at the door, shook my mother's hand, and then offered his hand to me. I don't recall having shaken anyone's hand before, but I did remember being told to grip the other person's hand firmly because a limp handshake was a major social *faux pas*. Oh, how I hoped I had held firmly enough.

Mr. Cobb offered us seats in his living room and asked if we would like coffee or a Coca Cola. Mom accepted the former and I the latter. While drinking her coffee Mom told him of our Georgia ties and they began discussing the state. Mrs. Cobb then passed through the room and introductions were made. Then she suggested, "Why don't you take the young man to the baseball room?"

"A fine suggestion," Mr. Cobb replied, and then to me, "Come along. Bring your drink."

We left the living room through a side door, went down a short hallway, and entered what I recall as a small paneled room with the entire left wall lined with shelves. A desk—dark, probably mahogany—was the main piece of furniture, but there were also a desk chair and an easy chair.

On the walls were several framed photographs, some of entire teams others of individuals. The shelves contained some books, but of much greater interest to me were old baseballs, a glove, more photos, and a few trophies. In the corner where the shelves met the outer wall were two bats, very much unlike the ones I used in Little League.

Mr. Cobb told me to have a seat and look at anything I wished; he would be back in a few minutes. He said he wanted to chat with Mom a while longer.

Unfortunately I don't recall all of the details of the items in the room—40 years is a long time—but I do remember a few things. One team picture was of the 1909 Tigers; when he returned Mr. Cobb told me about that team. There was a very old, very yellow baseball someone had signed. It was two names of average length, but I could not make out the letters and I never asked whose signature it was.

The bats were *very* heavy (for a 12-year-old, at least) and instead of the somewhat abrupt ends I was used to they tapered more gradually. The glove was very small, very flat, and very brittle. I put it on but could not close it; some oil would have worked wonders.

Other photos showed Mr. Cobb with other people, some with just one, others with two or more. A few were signed. Trophies have never held much interest for me and I'm not sure I read any of the engraving on the ones there.

After about 20 minutes or so he returned, apologizing for leaving me alone for so long. He asked if there was anything in particular I wanted to talk about and I cleverly replied, "Baseball!"

I'm sure there were portable recording devices available in 1953, but I was unaware of them and even if I had known about them I doubt that it would have occurred to me to have one with me. But, oh, how I wish I had.

Unfortunately I only recall bits and pieces of what he said. What I recall best, therefore I guess what impressed me the most, was his discussion of the 1909 Tigers. They were the best team in either league, he said, and should have won the World Series. He pointed to several faces in the team picture, identified them, and made comments. Some I had heard of, some I had not.

"Crawford," he said, "a quiet fellow. He was a gentleman, but we didn't always see eye-to-eye. He was a very powerful hitter."

"Schmidt. The catcher. Very slow but threw well. He had a very bad Series against Pittsburgh."

"Killian. Very talented but a nasty person."

"Mullin. Probaby the best pitcher in baseball that year. It was not his fault Pittsburgh beat us."

Ty Cobb (right) and author, 1953 (author's photo).

He spoke of three or four others, but what was said has long been forgotten. From that team picture he moved on to other photos.

He pointed to one of him and another man, square-jawed with what, although the photo was black-and-white, must have been grey or light blue eyes. The picture I assume was at least 25 or 30 years old then, but I remember thinking how little Cobb had changed. With a cap on in the photo, the hairline was hidden but the face had not changed (he did not look like a young man in the photo) and the baggy uniform made it difficult to evaluate his girth.

"That fellow is Walter Johnson, one of the finest gentlemen ever to play. I don't believe anyone ever threw faster. I've seen Bob Feller and that tall fellow who played for Cincinnati [Ewell Blackwell?] and many of the others over the years who had reputations for speed, but none could come near Johnson. There was one young fellow with Boston who was awfully fast, but he became injured and was not the same," he told me. I had no idea at the time who he meant, but now I believe he must have been referring to Smoky Joe Wood.

He pointed to another picture, one of him and four other men. Two men were in street clothes and in this photo Cobb was with the Athletics. He indicated one particular player. "That is Tris Speaker. Don't let anyone tell you I was not a good fielder; I was. But I could not compare to this man. Nor could anyone. The closest I have seen to him are the DiMaggio boys [I assume he meant Joe and Dom] and the Negro who played for the Giants but is now in the Army. [Mays?] But Speaker is the best."

He talked of other players in other pictures and of some who were not represented by photos. He spoke of Babe Ruth, "an amazingly graceful fellow [a word he used a lot] for one so huge." At that time Ruth had been dead for only a few years, and Mr. Cobb continued, "After his death, the writers were calling him the greatest ballplayer of all time, but these people never saw him play, or me. It is true that no one ever hit the ball harder, but he was not the greatest. In the 1930s when the idea for the Hall of Fame came up, the voters had seen us play. Both he and I had been retired for only a short while and I received more votes, more than Ruth or anyone. They saw me play and they agreed I was better." I guess Cobb's great ego had contributed to his tremendous success.

I remember a little more of what he said of himself: "The one thing that could be fairly criticized, I suppose, was my arm. Pitchers like to consider themselves good hitters, and likewise most hitters like to think they can pitch. I was like that. I would warm up before games as a pitcher, throwing—or attempting to throw—various trick pitches. But my arm suffered and I lost some strength in it."

We spoke more of his career, but I do not recall much. He thought no one would ever get as many hits or steal as many bases as he did. He was especially demeaning of modern ballplayers. "Fat and slow and only want home runs," was how he described them. With the exception of "the Negro," (an adjective he used whenever he mentioned a black player) "Minoso and one or two others, there is not a capable base stealer playing today."

He spoke more of modern ballplayers. "There are not many playing today who could have made much of a contribution in my day. Ted Williams spends more time flying than he does playing, but, young man, he would hit anywhere. He doesn't do other things too well, but he does hit."

I recall two others he mentioned as being able to play in the old days: Phil Rizzuto—"He goes about the game in the right manner," whatever that meant—and "that Negro Minoso, but obviously he wouldn't have been allowed to play." It was several years before I understood what he meant.

At this point, I asked him about my favorite players; could they have played in his day?

Eddie Yost? "A winning player, it's a shame he's with such a bad team."

Andy Pafko? "A good outfielder. He plays well."

Enos Slaughter? "Yes, indeed. Always on the go, always trying to win."

Elmer Valo? "He has the right attitude, but he might not hit well enough."

Ray Boone? "He's not a shortstop, but I see that he's playing third base." He had been traded to Detroit by Cleveland a few weeks earlier. "He's slow, but he appears to be a capable hitter."

I could have listened for hours, but it was nearly noon and Mom came back and said it was time to go. On the way out, I asked Mr. Cobb to sign my autograph book. I offered him a pen but he refused it, instead taking a fountain pen from his pocket and signing—in green ink—on the same page with such men as Bud Belardi, Larry Burgess, and Bill Marshall. Then he took my glove and signed it, too. The glove, unfortunately, has long since been lost, but the autograph book is still with me.

As he showed us out, I asked if I could take his picture. He consented and after I snapped him he said, "Give the camera to your mother and she can take one of us together." That had never occurred to me and, God, was that thrilling!

As we walked to the car, Cobb told Mom, "Bring him back sometime."

"Oh, Mr. Cobb," Mom replied, "that's very nice but we rarely come this way and it's a terrible imposition on you."

"Do you ever shop in San Francisco?" he asked. Shopping malls on every corner were still in the far distant future. "You can leave him here and pick him up on the way back."

"Please, Mom. Please, please!"

It was sort of left in the air, but about three weeks later Mom and a friend were going to San Francisco. I reminded her of what Mr. Cobb had said, and she rather reluctantly, it appeared, called him.

"Certainly. Bring him by," he told her.

My Brownie pictures had been developed and I took along the one I had taken of him outside his front door. I again took my glove.

Mom and her friend dropped me off around 9:30 in the morning, telling Mr. Cobb they would return in about three hours.

"There is no need to hurry," was his reply.

We talked more about baseball, and I learned for the first time that he had once managed the Tigers. He said he had been a successful manager even if he had not won a pennant.

After talking for about an hour, he took my glove and put it on. "If I had something like this, I would have caught everything," he said. (What would he have thought of today's gloves?) "Would you like to throw?"

"With you?"

"My wife doesn't play ball and no one else is here."

I could not believe it. He picked up his old, flat, little glove from the shelf and an old, unround, yellow (almost brown) ball, and said, "We'll go out to the side of the house; there's more room there." He had been wearing a sports jacket, which he now took off, and we headed outside. A few minutes later, Mrs. Cobb came out. She was a small, thin, angular, dark-haired woman who kept a low profile while I was there; this was only the second time I had seen her. "Be careful! I'm going out and I don't want to return to a broken arm," she said. He assured her all would be well.

We started throwing about 25 feet apart and he dropped several at first, but after about ten minutes his arm and glove both seemed to limber up. We moved back to about 45 to 50 feet and he began throwing as hard as I wanted to receive and urging me to throw as hard to him. We both made several errant throws but continued for probably a half hour. Finally he called it a day, saying, "My mind still has the ability of a young man, but my body is reminding me that it's been around for over 60 years. Tomorrow I shall wonder why I did this today."

It was lunch time and Mom had not yet reappeared. "I think we have some cold meat; may I make you a sandwich?" he asked. Of course I agreed. It seemed that he was not overly familiar with the kitchen; he could find no mayonnaise so we had mustard on our bologna (I think) sandwiches. He gave me another Coke but I think he drank water; for dessert he gave me Oreos. I had never cared for Oreos (I don't like chocolate) but I did not say so to him and he said he was not much of a cookie eater.

These, it seemed, belonged to the woman who periodically cleaned the house.

Shortly after lunch, Mom came for me. The snapshot I had taken was in the car; I got it and asked him to autograph it. Again he refused my pen and used his green ink fountain pen.

As we were walking to the car, he again said for Mom to bring me back. It was late August, however, and Mother told him school would be starting soon and it would probably not be possible. "Well, any time is fine," he said and shook my hand. I again wondered if my grip was firm enough.

* * *

I never saw Ty Cobb again. School prevented it until the next summer, and by then my mother had begun selling real estate and I had no transportation. I asked once and she told me that it just did not seem possible.

Somehow I assumed he would always live in Atherton and I could go back someday. That was not to be, however. Several years later, when I had practically become an adult, I read of his death in Atlanta. I was very sad that I had never made it back to see him again.

Tyrus Raymond (The Georgia Peach) Cobb

Born December 18, 1886, Narrows, GA
Died July 17, 1961, Atlanta, GA
Ht. 6′1″ Wt. 175 Batted Left and Threw Right

Year	Team	G	AB	R	H	2B	3B	HR	RBI	SB	BA	SA
1905	DetA	41	150	19	36	6	0	1	15	2	.240	.300
1906		98	350	45	112	13	7	1	41	23	.320	.406
1907		150	605	97	212*	29	15	5	116*	49*	.350*	.473*
1908		150	581	88	188*	36*	20*	4	108*	39	.324*	.475*
1909		156*	573	116*	216*	33	10	9*	107*	76*	.377*	.517*
1910		140	509	106*	196	36	13	8	91	65	.385*	.554*
1911		146	591	147*	248*	47*	24*	8	144*	83*	.420*	.621*
1912		140	553	119	227*	30	23	7	90	61	.410*	.586*
1913		122	428	70	167	18	16	4	67	52	.390*	.535
1914		97	345	69	127	22	11	2	57	35	.368*	.513*
1915		156*	563	144*	208*	31	13	3	99	96*	.369*	.487
1916		145	542	113*	201	31	10	5	68	68*	.371	.493
1917		152	588*	107	225*	44*	23*	7	102	55*	.383*	.571*
1918		111	421	83	161	19	14*	3	64	34	.382*	.515
1919		124	497	92	191*	36	13	1	70	28	.384*	.515

Year	Team	G	AB	R	H	2B	3B	HR	RBI	SB	BA	SA
1920		112	428	86	143	28	8	2	63	14	.334	.451
1921		128	507	124	197	37	16	12	101	22	.389	.596
1922		137	526	99	211	42	16	4	99	9	.401	.565
1923		145	556	103	189	40	7	6	88	9	.340	.469
1924		155*	625	115	211	38	10	4	74	23	.338	.450
1925		121	415	97	157	31	12	12	102	13	.378	.598
1926		79	233	48	79	18	5	4	62	9	.339	.511
1927	PhiA	134	490	104	175	32	7	5	93	22	.357	.482
1928		95	353	54	114	27	4	1	40	5	.323	.431
24 years		3034	11429	2245	4191	724	297	118	1961	892	.367	.513

**Led League*

World Series

Year	Team	G	AB	R	H	2B	3B	HR	RBI	SB	BA	SA
1907	DetA	5	20	1	4	0	1	0	1	0	.200	.300
1908		5	19	3	7	1	0	0	4	2	.368	.421
1909		7	26	3	6	3	0	0	6	2	.231	.346
3 years		17	65	7	17	4	1	0	11	4	.262	.354

PITCHING RECORD

Year	Team	G	IP	W	L	PCT	BB	SO	H	SHO	SV	ERA
1918	DetA	2	4	0	0	.000	2	0	6	0	0	4.50
1925		1	1	0	0	.000	0	0	0	0	1	0.00
2 years		3	5	0	0	.000	2	0	6	0	1	3.60

BILL ROGELL

Infield of Dreams

1925–1940

The Tigers of the mid– to late–1930s had some excellent players and fielded some excellent teams. After three straight American League pennants in 1907, 1908 and 1909, the club settled in for a quarter century of mediocrity, rarely being a bad team but never being a good team. By the 1930s, the Tigers were on their way back.

Above: **Bill Rogell (courtesy Detroit Tigers).**

Their climb back to the top probably began in 1926. That was the year Charlie Gehringer became the second baseman. But it was not a rapid climb. The next step did not occur until 1932, when Billy Rogell became the everyday shortstop. Also, in 1932, Gee Walker took over in center field for his brother, Hub.

Three more additions came in 1933: Marv Owen, a rookie in 1931 but a minor leaguer in 1932, became the third baseman; and two rookies, Hank Greenberg and Pete Fox, blossomed at first base and center field, respectively. Gee Walker was moved to right to make way for Fox.

The pitching staff had been changing, also. Tommy Bridges joined the rotation in 1931 and Schoolboy Rowe in 1933. Firpo Marberry and Carl Fischer were acquired for Earl Whitehill in 1933. Elden Auker joined them in mid–1933.

Then in December 1933 two deals were made. In both, the Tigers acquired a Hall of Famer and the addition of these two turned the fifth-place team of 1933 into American League champions. On December 12, Detroit sent minor league catcher Johnny Pasek and $100,000 to Connie Mack's Philadelphia Athletics for Mickey Cochrane. Cochrane was named manager, replacing Del Baker who had replaced Bucky Harris at the end of 1933. He also replaced Ray Hayworth behind the plate. Then on December 20, John Stone, a fixture in the outfield since 1930, was traded to the Washington Senators for Goose Goslin. The Goose's better days were behind him, but he could still bat .300 and drive in 100 runs.

As the 1934 season began Jo Jo White, a reserve in the previous years, was made the regular center fielder. Walker ended up platooning with both White and Fox in center and right. The team which had finished in fifth place in 1933 was suddenly a force to be reckoned with. Only one more addition was needed.

General Crowder had led the league in wins the two previous years (with 26 in 1932 and 24 in 1933) for the Senators, but in 1934 he was struggling (4-10, 6.77). On August 4, he was put on waivers and Detroit claimed him. He took over for veteran Vic Sorrell in the rotation and went 5-1 the rest of the way.

The team ended up with 101 wins, a new franchise record, and beat the second-place Yankees by seven games. And, even though other Tiger squads have won as many or more games (101 in 1961, 103 in 1968, 104 in 1984), 1934's winning percentage of .656 remains the tops in team history.

In 1935, the same line-up won again and this time they were World Champions. They started very badly, actually dropping into the cellar, but staged a late-season comeback to win 93 games and finish three up on the Yankees. Again a late-season pitching addition helped—Roxie Lawson was

3-1 in four starts (with two shutouts) and had two saves in three relief efforts.

In 1934, Cochrane was the league's MVP and in 1935 it was Greenberg. Both years the team led the league in batting (.300 in 1934 and .290 in 1935) and was second in ERA.

Here are the line-ups and batting averages for the two years:

		1934		1935
Hank Greenberg, 1b		.339		.328
Charlie Gehringer, 2b		.356		.330
Billy Rogell, ss		.296		.275
Marv Owen, 3b		.317		.263
Pete Fox, rf		.285		.321
Jo Jo White, cf		.313		.240
Goose Goslin, lf		.305		.292
Mickey Cochrane, c		.320		.319
Gee Walker, of	347 at bats	.300	362 at bats	.301
Ray Hayworth, c	167 at bats	.293	175 at bats	.309
Schoolboy Rowe, p	103 at bats	.303	109 at bats	.312

The infield was especially productive. In 1934 the four set a record for RBIs by an infield with 462 (Greenberg 139, Gehringer 127, Rogell 100, Owen 96). Goslin, also, knocked in 100.

The infield drove in 420 runs in 1935 (Greenberg 170, Gehringer 108, Rogell 71, Owen 71) and Goslin added 109.

And the pitchers won consistently:

	1934		1935
Schoolboy Rowe	24- 8		19-13
Tommy Bridges	22-11		21-10
Eldon Auker	15- 7		18- 7
General Crowder	5- 1		16-10
Firpo Marberry	15- 5	Roxie Lawson	3- 1

The team finished second in both 1936 and 1937. Both years two key men went down to injuries. In 1936, Greenberg's wrist injury incurred in the 1935 Series was not properly healed and he appeared in only 12 games and Cochrane's health limited him to 44 games. At one point Cochrane went to Wyoming to recuperate. Bridges led the league with 23 wins and Rowe added 19, but Crowder got old (he was 38) and Lawson could only manage eight wins with a 5.48 ERA. Though they batted .300 again, the 1936 Tigers finished 19½ games behind the Yankees.

The three-quarters of the infield that remained sound again produced well (Gehringer .354, 116 RBIs; Rogell .274, 68 RBIs; Owen .295, 105 RBIs) as did Goslin (.315, 125), Walker (.353, 93), and Al Simmons (.327, 112), who had been purchased the previous December and took over for White in center. But Jack Burns was not Greenberg and Hayworth was not Cochrane.

In 1937 two more injuries kept the Tigers in second, 13 games out this time. A beaning nearly killed Cochrane, ending his career, and Rowe, who had won 62 games in the previous three years, won only one game and his ailing arm put his future in doubt.

Simmons, for whom the Tigers had paid $75,000, was sold to Washington for only $15,000 just before the season opener and Goslin aged overnight. Fox (.331) and Walker (.335, 113 RBIs) responded to the challenge and White regained his spot in center, although rookie Chet Laabs saw a lot of time there too.

The infield returned to its 400-RBI level (432), although a league-leading 183 came from Greenberg and it took five players instead of four to accomplish it. Rookie Rudy York split his time between catcher (51 games) and third base (44). Offensively he was magnificent (.307, 35 home runs, 103 RBIs), but he was a defensive liability at both positions. Gehringer's .371 batting average led the league, as did the team's .292, giving them a four-year average of .296.

The pitching, though, was nothing like it had been. The team ERA (4.87) was seventh in the league. Lawson bounced back to go 18-7, but he had a 5.27 ERA. Auker (17-9, 3.88) and Bridges (15-12, 4.08) pitched well and rookies George Gill (11-4) and Boots Poffenberger (10-5) also contributed, but the loss of Rowe was disastrous.

In those four years, 1934 through 1937, the Tigers did everything well. Although they never had the league leader, as a team they led in stolen bases in 1934 and finished second in 1935 and 1937 and third in 1936.

And they were far and away the top fielding team in the American League. They were tops in the league in 1935, 1936, and 1937 and finished second by .0002 in 1934. Rarely in the history of the game has a team shown such fielding consistency for so many years.

The infield was especially sound with the glove. Gehringer accounted for the league lead in nine departments over the four years, Rogell five, Owen four, and Greenberg two. Fox, Simmons, and Rowe each had one league-leading fielding statistic.

When healthy, this was a team with no weak spot.

But by 1938 the team was breaking up. Goslin, Owen, White, and Walker were either gone or benched, and Rowe still had not recovered. In 1938, they dropped to fourth place.

But four of the regulars from the two Series teams are in the Hall of Fame, and from 1934 through 1937 this was one of the greatest groups of ballplayers ever assembled. Billy Rogell, the Tigers' shortstop from 1932 through 1938, thinks so, too.

*   *   *

BK: In 1925 you came to the majors with the Red Sox, a very bad team. You were only 20 years old. What was your minor league experience?

BILL ROGELL: I had a year-and-a-half in the minor leagues. I did all right.

The first year I went to Coffeyville, Kansas, in the old Southwestern League and the league blew up after about six weeks. Then I went back to live with a sister in Chicago and the next year I went to Salina [Kansas] and I hit .317 that year and the Red Sox bought me.

Then I went to Jersey City in '26 and I did good.

BK: In your younger days you were very versatile; you played both infield and outfield.

BR: When I went to Coffeyville in '23, the manager of the ballclub was the second baseman. I was originally a second baseman and I couldn't very well take the manager out of there so they put me in the outfield. I played about seven or eight games and we played a game over in Sapulpa, Oklahoma, and I ran into a daggone fence and busted three ribs. That ended my baseball career as an outfielder.

BK: When did you become a full-time shortstop?

BR: Really and truly, when I became full-time was when I went to St. Paul in '29. That was an old Yankee farm and the Tigers bought me from there.

Ben Chapman and I were on the same club together; he played third and I played short.

BK: I didn't realize he was ever an infielder.

BR: Oh, yes. He played third base.

I remember very well when he cut Gehringer in New York. He spiked him. I told him, I said, "Ben, remember when you played third base, whenever anyone slid hard into you, you raised hell. Now you're an outfielder and you think you're going to tear the infield apart: Let me tell you something, Buddy, don't come into me that way 'cause I'll kick you right in the teeth!" And I did!

BK: How did the Tigers acquire you?

BR: When I played at St. Paul the owner of the ballclub came to me and said, "Five big league ballclubs are after you." I hit .336 that year. I played second, I played short, I played third—I played all of 'em because of injuries. He asked me, "Where would you like to go?"

I said, "What clubs are after me?"

He says, "The Phils, Pittsburgh, Detroit Tigers, White Sox, and Yankees."

"Detroit," I said. "That's where I want to go." For some reason, I always liked Detroit. I could have gone to the Yankees, but I wanted to go to Detroit and I'm glad I did because I was there 40 years as a [city] councilman.

I think I did a lot for that city. I was chairman of the committee that built that big airport there. Also the roads and bridges committee.

BK: You were a better hitter when you joined the Tigers.

BR: I was always a good hitter. When I went to Boston in 1925 they tried to make a righthanded hitter out of me because of that left field wall. They just screwed me up for a couple of years.

BK: For a six or seven year period, from the early '30s to the late '30s, you were as good a shortstop as there was. You led in fielding average three times, in double plays twice, and in putouts and assists. I guess it helped that you had a pretty good second baseman next to you.

BR: I had one of the best. None better. I've seen 'em all; I saw Eddie Collins, I saw [Rogers] Hornsby and [Frankie] Frisch and all of 'em and he was the best.

There were a lot of good ones, don't get me wrong. Let me tell you this: I played the game for 20 years practically; there's not that much difference between the superstars and the *real* good ballplayers. It all depends on whether you've got a real good newspaper boy back of you, you know? He can really make a star out of you.

But Gehringer didn't have to take a back seat to anybody. Nobody. He could hit and field and he could run. The only trouble—Charlie hurt his arm and he never was a double play man. If he had the arm he *used* to have, I think we could have broken double play records like nobody's business. Really.

BK: Tell me about the Tigers infield of '34. You guys set the RBI record for an infield. Owen at third had 96 and the rest of you guys had over 100.

BR: We drove in 462. It's never been beaten. And again in '35 we drove in over 400 runs.

It's a funny thing. When the writers write about the great teams they

"Infield of Dreams" (*left to right*: Greenberg, Gehringer, Rogell, Owen) (courtesy Elmer D. Kapp).

never write about the Tigers of '34 and '35. We were as good as any ballclub; I don't care which one you talk about.

We had a great outfield and a great infield. We had one of the greatest catchers in the world. We had four men who went to the Hall of Fame. And great pitching.

And still we never get recognition. Even Jim Campbell of the Tigers didn't know we drove in 462 runs. You really need publicity.

BK: You had some great ballplayers in those years and they aren't remembered now.

BR: Oh, yes. Don't think I'm silly now. Pee Wee Reese and this guy from South America [Luis Aparicio] are in the big Hall of Fame. If they were better than I was, they've got to show it.

BK: Pretty much the only difference between you and them is in stolen bases.

BR: I led off most of my baseball career and they didn't want me to steal. I had Gehringer and Cochrane and Greenberg hitting behind me. We did a lot of hitting and running.

Now these guys today, these rabbits they've got playing baseball, they get four runs behind or ten runs ahead and they keep running. The artificial turf helps the runners.

Fielding has changed, too. You just don't get bad bounces today. I can truly say 98 percent of your players today couldn't play in the big leagues back in those days.

And they were better hitters then, too.

BK: Hal Newhouser is the only pitcher who spent any time with the Tigers who is in the Hall of Fame.

BR: Yes, and we had some good ones. Tommy Bridges was a wonderful guy. Great curveball. A hell of a nice guy.

Ray Hayworth, our second string catcher, was a wonderful guy, too. He was good enough to be first string, but we had Mickey Cochrane. They don't have any catchers today. I think the major leagues today are like Triple-A or Double-A baseball in my day.

BK: Do you think it's dilution—too many teams and too many players?

BR: I'm not a racist, but remember when I played we had no blacks, no Puerto Ricans, no nothing. All white boys. And after the war everything changed. The blacks and all added power and if they're good enough to play, they should.

But they're not as close as we were. We rode in trains; today they fly. They play, they go home, they don't see their teammates till the next game. We were on trains. We sat there and talked baseball—how do you pitch to this guy, how's this guy hit. Today they're not interested. They can't be.

We had two coaches—first base coach, third base coach. That's all we had. Today they've got experts for everything—infield coach, catching coach, help for the manager. When a guy gets to the big leagues he's supposed to know baseball. You don't need that much coaching.

In my day, you get in a slump you worked it out yourself. Today they've got eight guys watching you and you still hit only .230.

They get too much money today—they don't know what to do with it. They say the owners can afford it. Hell, more power to 'em.

I played in the majors 14 years—I don't get a pension. You know what these guys are going to get? They're going to get $96,000 a year—$8,000 a month—when they retire at 62. And some of these guys are making millions today.

Us poor bastards that made the game for 'em—we get nothing.

The players today don't know the old players. The only one they know is Babe Ruth, but nobody else.

BK: The Tigers were back-to-back American League champions in '34 and '35. You lost the Series in '34.

BR: An American League umpire cost us that Series. Brick Owen called Mickey out at third base on Goslin's bunt. I was the next hitter 'cause I was batting fifth. I hit a long fly ball to center and the man went from second to third. Greenberg follows me with a single and there's only one out.

The next guy flies out and that would've scored another run. We should've scored three runs that inning instead of one. They beat us, 4 to 3, so we shoulda beat them, 5 to 4. But that's water over the dam.

I played on a fractured ankle in the '34 Series. I hit Dizzy [Dean] good, but I couldn't hit Paul. Paul didn't have half what Dizzy had.

BK: You came back and won it the next year.

BR: Yep, we beat a better ballclub than the Cardinals.

We won in '35 against the Cubs and we lost Greenberg in the first game with a broken wrist. I can truthfully say that the '35 Cubs were a lot better ballclub than the Cardinals of '34. And we beat 'em with Owen at first and Flea Clifton at third.

BK: You had the same ballclub both years.

BR: That's right. Remember, we lost Rowe and Mickey Cochrane and we still finished second the next two years. You can't lose a 24-game pitcher and the best catcher in baseball and expect to win.

Even then, with our pitching staff—Rowe, Bridges, Auker, Crowder—we needed one more pitcher. If we'd had one more, even though we lost Rowe and Mickey, we'd have won that thing four years in a row.

We had the ballclub—we could run, hit the ball, field it.

Let me repeat, I still can't get over that nobody recognizes our ballclub of '34 and '35!

BK: Who was the best hitter you ever saw?

BR: The best? Ty Cobb. No, Shoeless Joe Jackson was the best I ever saw. I'll tell you one thing, if they let this guy from Cincinnati back, they ought to put Jackson back.

BK: The best all-around player?

BR: George Sisler. He was a first baseman; of course, each position would be different. He was a hell of a hitter and a hell of a fielder. He's the guy I like.

Now take that boy that played ball for the Giants—Lefty O'Doul. Here's a guy who hit .349 lifetime, led the National League a couple years, and he doesn't even get in the Hall of Fame. He doesn't even get on the list.

A lot of people ask why nobody recommends me for the big Hall of Fame. I say, "Well, Gehringer's on the Old-Timers [Committee]." "Why doesn't he place your name in?" I say, "You go ask him." Maybe he doesn't think I was that good. He made me and I helped make him.

He's only one man, but [Ted] Williams got his second baseman [Bobby Doerr] in. And he tried to get [Phil] Rizzuto in.

Year	Team	G	AB	R	H	2B	3B	HR	RBI	SB	BA	SA
1930	DetA	54	144	20	24	4	2	0	9	1	.167	.222
1931		48	185	21	56	12	3	2	24	8	.303	.432
1932		143	554	88	150	29	6	9	61	14	.271	.394
1933		155	587	67	173	42	11	0	57	6	.295	.404
1934		154	592	114	175	32	8	3	100	13	.296	.392
1935		150	560	88	154	23	11	6	71	3	.275	.388
1936		146	585	85	160	27	5	6	68	14	.274	.368
1937		146	536	83	148	30	7	8	64	5	.276	.403
1938		136	501	86	130	22	8	3	55	9	.259	.353
1939		74	174	24	40	6	3	2	23	3	.230	.333
1940	ChiN	33	59	7	8	0	0	1	3	1	.156	.186
14 years		1481	5149	755	1375	256	75	42	609	82	.267	.370

World Series

Year	Team	G	AB	R	H	2B	3B	HR	RBI	SB	BA	SA
1934	DetA	7	29	3	8	1	0	0	4	0	.276	.310
1935		6	24	1	7	2	0	0	1	0	.292	.375
2 years		13	53	4	15	3	0	0	5	0	.283	.340

RAY BENGE

Stuck in the Second Division

1925–1938

You can usually look at a batter's record and tell something about his performance and ability. If his batting average is .340, you *know* he can hit. If he hits 37 home runs, you *know* he has power.

But it's a lot more difficult to look at a pitcher's stats and determine the quality of his performance. You see 18 wins and you think, "Good year." You see 12 wins and you think, "Well, he's okay." Eight wins, "Not so hot."

***Above:* Ray Benge (George Brace photo).**

Earned run average is the same. 3.20 is "good," 4.34 is not.

Pitching, though, far more than hitting, is affected by what else the team has. Eighteen wins on a pennant-winning 100-victory team may not be as impressive as 12 wins on a cellar-dweller which wins only 58. An ERA of 3.20 on a staff with an ERA of 3.46 is not as good as a 4.34 on a 5.16 staff.

The biggest thing to affect a pitcher's record is not hitting (or lack of same), although that certainly figures in. It's fielding. A lot of errors certainly can be a problem, but throughout the years that has not been as important as range.

Etch this in stone somewhere. Range is the most important fielding consideration. It may be *the* most important statistic of all. Simply, if a fielder cannot move enough to get to a ball, he *cannot* field it. The result is scored as a base hit and eventually these led to runs. Lots of runs. *Earned* runs.

Now if you want really horrendous results, couple poor range with bad hands and weak arms. Not only do the fielders not get to as many balls as their counterparts on other teams, those they do reach they cannot handle.

This pretty much describes the support Ray Benge received in the late 1920s and 1930s with the Phillies and Dodgers. These were generally good-hitting ballclubs, especially the Phils. Usually the teams would score runs, but poor fielding and mediocre pitching resulted in a low finish in the standings.

That brings us to another thing affecting a pitcher's record. When a staff has no depth, one of two things results when the start tires: He stays in because there is no one who would be any more effective to relieve him or a reliever is brought in who could not get Great Aunt Susie out.

That fairly well describes what Ray Benge was up against throughout his career. He spent nine full seasons (1928–36) in the National League with Philadelphia, Brooklyn, and Boston. Only once did his club finish in the first division and only once did his club have a .500 record—78-76 in 1932 with the Phillies. Despite this, Ray won in double figures six times and consistently pitched better than his team. For those nine years, Benge's winning percentage was .432; that of his teams, .419. His ERA was 4.54; his teams, 4.92.

From 1929 through 1934, the National League had some great pitchers. Hall of Famers Burleigh Grimes, Carl Hubbell, Jesse Haines, Eppa Rixey, and Dazzy Vance were active during those years, along with such top-flight hurlers as Freddie Fitzsimmons, Guy Bush, Ray Kremer, Red Lucas, and Pat Malone. Only six men won in double figures for that period, and one of them was Ray Benge. He did it despite the fact the average finish for his team was sixth place.

Ray Benge is over 90 now. He is one of the last around who pitched to such greats as Babe Ruth, Lou Gehrig, Al Simmons, Hack Wilson, Mel Ott, the Waners, Frankie Frisch, Kiki Cuyler, Rogers Hornsby, and Chick Hafey, and on and on. Even against these kind of hitters, he held his own.

* * *

BK: Who signed you originally?

RAY BENGE: Oh, my goodness gracious. That was a long time ago. It was probably Houston. The Houston Buffs. I played there one year.

BK: You came to the majors at the end of the 1925 season with Cleveland and pitched a shutout in your first start.

RB: I think it was against Philadelphia. [It was, on September 26, 1925; 6–0.] I know I pitched against Babe Ruth [in another game that season].

BK: The main part of your career was spent in the National League with the Phillies. How did they get you?

RB: I was playing with Peoria, I believe. The Cleveland Indians sent me down there and Philadelphia bought me from there.

BK: In your nine full seasons in the National League you only played for one winning team. You had the misfortune to be on a very bad bunch of teams. How bad were the Phillies in those days?

RB: Well, they were good in some places but most of the players didn't come to par with the other teams. They just needed two or three or four players in different places here and there and they'd have been a good ballclub.

BK: You had very little help on the pitching staff.

RB: That's right. I always felt if I pitched like I did and been on a better ballclub I'd have won a lot more games. The backup for the pitchers—the support—wasn't too strong. No one to come in.

BK: You were a pretty fair hitter.

RB: (Laughs) Well, I would swing and the ball happened to be in there.

BK: You hit a home run.

RB: Yeah, that was in Philadelphia. I was with Brooklyn but was in the Philadelphia ballpark. It had to be because they had such a short right field there. I forget the distance from home plate to the right field fence but, gosh, it wasn't far, about three times the distance from home to first base. If you hit the ball high, a high pop-up in right field, the outfielders would have to come in after it in a regular ballpark but in this one it would drop over it [the fence].

Ray Benge (courtesy National Pastime).

There was a real high fence up there. They had a solid fence up about 30 to 35 feet, then they had a screen way up on top of that. A hard hit ball would hit that and drop and be a double or single. The right field wall was almost right back of first base. There was some awfully good games pitched in that park. [This is the infamous Baker Bowl.]

BK: Is there one game that stands out?

RB: I pitched a lot of good ballgames, low-scoring games, but to go back and pick out one, I can't. I had a one-hitter against somebody, but I just can't recall that right now.

BK: Let's talk about some of the players you played with or against. Lefty O'Doul.

RB: He was a good one.

BK: A lot of people feel he belongs in the Hall of Fame.

RB: (Laughs) As far as I'm concerned, he does.

BK: Chuck Klein.

RB: He's another good one. He won the Triple Crown when I was there.

Chuck was an extra good hitter. What I mean, if the ball was over the outside of the plate or something like that it would be almost the same as if it was right down through the middle. He'd hit it.

BK: Buzz Arlett—he was a minor league legend but had a questionable glove. Do you remember him?

RB: Just slightly. He wasn't quite good enough to be a regular. He hit well.

[Arlett was a hitting machine in the minors. Originally signed as a pitcher—he won 20 three times—by Oakland of the PCL in 1918, he switched to the outfield in 1923. In 19 minor league seasons, he walloped 432 home runs, drove in 1,786, and batted .341. In his only major league season, 1931 with the Phillies, he hit 18 home runs and drove in 72 with a .313 average. Defense was his shortcoming, but in spite of that SABR members voted him the outstanding minor leaguer of all time.]

BK: Babe Herman—you never played with him but you played against him for years. He was a marvelous hitter but also had some trouble with the glove.

RB: Yeah, he did. He was one of those that when it was his time to come to the plate you wished it was somebody else.

BK: Hall of Fame?

RB: I would vote for it.

BK: Your catcher in Brooklyn was Al Lopez. Was he the best you saw behind the plate?

RB: Yep. He was good. He was a good leader.

BK: Who was the best player you saw?

RB: It was on the tail-end of his career, but I've still got to say it. It has to be Babe Ruth. He hit a home run off of me. It was just one. I don't know how many times I pitched to him, not a heck of a lot. I remember the one he hit off of me. Al Lopez was catching.

Right field, you know, at Boston was kinda short. The right field bleachers were right on the line. Al was catching and he said, "Let's pitch this guy inside and see if he can hit a home run." (Laughs) And believe it or not, he did it. That son of a gun hit that ball right straight back over my head, right over the center field fence, the longest place in that park. A little over 400 feet, I think.

We were ahead of 'em, 8 to 1 or 8 to nothing, something like that, and Lopez came out there and said let's see what he can do. (Laughs)

BK: Who was the best pitcher?

RB: Oh, you've got a basketful.

BK: Van Lingle Mungo was with you in Brooklyn.

RB: If he'd have had a little bit better control, he would have *really* been tough. He was pretty tough as it was, but he would just rear back and throw. I don't know how you could time it unless you had a quick watch.

BK: Did you save souvenirs from your career?

RB: I really had some souvenirs. I had a scrapbook from the beginning to the end, signed balls, and I don't know what all, but somebody liked it a heck of a lot better than I did because it disappeared. The whole works. Not one thing do I have left.

I had it in the car, you see, and I was going to some friends' house. They wanted me to bring the stuff that was easy to carry so they could look at it. I left it in the car for a little while when I went in and I guess I stayed in a little bit longer than I thought. When I went back out there wasn't a single thing left. I put it in the Houston papers and all over. I offered a $500 reward if somebody just let me know *where* it was.

BK: Do you still get fan mail?

RB: It really isn't fan mail; I get stuff to autograph. Pictures or just a piece of paper. If they send it, I sign it.

BK: People see your record in the book and see you were a pretty good pitcher and want your autograph.

RB: Most of the people, not all of 'em, don't know the meaning of all of it. They see the losing record and think, "Just another ballplayer."

That team had some good hitters on it. Other pitchers were just doggone particular how they pitched to them.

BK: Would you go back and do it again?

RB: I certainly would. I enjoyed it.

BK: Any regrets?

RB: No. I just wished I could have been with a better club. Everybody does that. There wouldn't be any baseball clubs if everybody was on the best. (Laughs) Even the bottom club, when you come right down to it, they're a heck of a ballclub. They're not a bad ballclub. You got to be good to play in the major leagues.

Raymond Adelphia (Silent Cal) Benge

Born April 22, 1902, Jacksonville, TX
Ht. 5′9½″ Wt. 160 Batted and Threw Right

Year	Team	G	IP	W	L	PCT	BB	SO	H	SHO	SV	ERA
1925	CleA	2	11.2	1	0	1.000	3	3	9	1	0	1.54
1926		8	11.2	1	0	1.000	4	3	15	0	0	3.86
1928	PhiN	40	201.2	8	18	.308	88	68	219	1	1	4.55
1929		38	199	11	15	.423	77	78	255	2	4	6.29
1930		38	225.2	11	15	.423	81	70	305	0	1	5.70
1931		38	247	14	18	.438	61	117	251	2	2	3.17
1932		41	222.1	13	12	.520	58	89	247	2	6	4.05
1933	BrkN	37	228.2	10	17	.370	55	74	238	2	1	3.42
1934		36	227	14	12	.538	61	64	252	1	0	4.32
1935		23	124.2	9	9	.500	47	39	142	1	1	4.48
1936	BosN	21	115	7	9	.438	38	32	161	0	0	5.79
	PhiN	15	45.2	1	4	.200	19	13	70	0	1	4.73
1938	CinN	9	15.1	1	1	.500	6	5	13	0	2	4.11
12 years		346	1875.1	101	130	.437	598	655	2177	12	19	4.52

CLYDE SUKEFORTH

Baseball History
1926–1945

Many people have spent years in baseball and never been a part of history-making events. Really historic events in any endeavor are not common and there just are not enough to go around for everyone to be part of. So when a man is integral in not one but *four* of baseball's biggest events, he's something special. Clyde Sukeforth is one of those special men.

Above: **Clyde Sukeforth (George Brace photo).**

Sukeforth signed with the Reds out of Georgetown University in 1925, but after one appearance as a pinch hitter (a strikeout) he was sent down. The next year he was up to stay and by 1929 was the Reds' number one receiver. From then through the 1931 season, as the regular backstop, he batted .292.

But then he was sent to Brooklyn in the trade that brought Hall of Famer Ernie Lombardi to Cincinnati. The reason the Dodgers swapped Lombardi was still there, though, and for the next several years Clyde was the backup to an other future HOFer, Al Lopez.

In 1936 he began a seven-year minor league managerial career, never having a losing season and ending up with a .555 winning percent. In 1943 he returned to the Dodgers as a coach/scout and stayed there through 1951, when he accompanied Branch Rickey to the Pirates.

Now for Clyde Sukeforth's places in history.

1. In 1945 Rickey sent Sukeforth to Chicago to see a shortstop with the Kansas City Monarchs named Jackie Robinson. His instructions were to bring him to Brooklyn.

2. Brooklyn manager Leo Durocher was suspended just prior to the beginning of the 1947 season, leaving the Dodgers temporarily without a skipper. Rickey decided that Burt Shotton would guide the team but Shotton had to be brought to Brooklyn from his home in Florida, where he had retired. The season would open before Shotton could arrive, so Rickey directed his coaching staff to decide among themselves who would lead the team until Shotton's arrival. Sukeforth was chosen and thus became Jackie Robinson's first major league manager.

3. On October 3, 1951, Sukeforth was in the bullpen in the Polo Grounds observing the Dodger relief pitchers as they warmed up. There were three: Carl Erskine, who had pitched the day before and whose arm was bothering him; Clem Labine, whose ankles needed to be taped when he pitched and who did not even have his shoes on; and Ralph Branca, who was throwing pretty well. Sukeforth told manager Charlie Dressen that there was nothing wrong with Branca, so when the time came he got the call to pitch to Bobby Thomson. The "Shot Heard 'Round the World" was the result. Dressen, who was once given a book by his players on which every page was the letter "I," did not take the credit this time. "Sukeforth said to use Branca," he said.

4. In 1954—Sukeforth and Rickey were now with the Pirates—Rickey sent Sukeforth to Richmond to watch a five-game series between the Virginians and the Montreal Royals, the top Dodger farm team. Rickey wanted a report on pitcher Joe Black. Should the Pirates consider drafting him? Black did not pitch but Sukeforth came back to Rickey with a draft recom-

mendation anyhow: a 20-year-old Puerto Rican outfielder named Roberto Clemente.

Clyde Sukeforth is out of baseball now. He's over 90 now, still lives in rural Maine and is still active. The first time I called him he was out. "You won't be able to reach him in the mornings," his wife told me. "He goes hunting every day."

* * *

BK: You didn't play professionally until you were 24.

CLYDE SUKEFORTH: I was raised up in Washington, Maine, back in the early part of this century. It was very rural and my sister and I walked three-and-a-half miles a day, each way, to a one-room, one-teacher, so-called high school. After four years you had acquired enough units—credits—to put you into the junior year of an accredited school, so I went from there up to Coldbrook Classical Institute in Waterville. Naturally, I got a slow start.

BK: You went to college for a couple of years.

CS: Yeah. I went to Georgetown for a couple years. I was there in '23-4 and '4-5 and at the end of the '25 year I signed with Cincinnati—in the fall of '25. Tommy Whalen was the scout.

BK: You came to the majors as a reserve but in 1929 you batted .354 as the regular catcher.

CS: Yeah, I legged a few.

Bubbles Hargrave led the National League in hitting in 1926. That was my first year there and they optioned me out. He was there again in '27 and the only time I got to play was if Bubbles got a base hit in the late innings, why I'd go in and run for him and get to bat once possibly. If I hit a ball good I couldn't reach those fences in Cincinnati, so I choked up and became a contact hitter. I legged a few in '29 and '30. I think I wound up around .260-something for lifetime.

BK: Cincinnati had a fine bunch of pitchers.

CS: [Dolf] Luque, Pete Donahue, Jakie May, Carl Mays, [Eppa] Rixey, [Red] Lucas. Yeah, we had good pitchin' but we didn't score any runs. We had hitters like me. (Laughs)

BK: You had Harvey Hendrick. He could hit.

CS: Yeah, he was a pretty good hitter. He came afterwards. At one time, we had Wally Pipp and George Kelly.

BK: Leo Durocher was the shortstop there in Cincinnati and later you coached under him at Brooklyn. Does he belong in the Hall of Fame?

CS: Personally, I think he belongs there. Leo was a good manager. [Durocher was elected to the Hall of Fame in 1993.]

BK: How did you feel about being traded to Brooklyn in 1932?

CS: I'd gotten shot through my right eye in the fall of '31 and I really regretted that the trade hadn't been made before. I don't use that for an alibi—I mean, I can see out of the right eye but I can't read newspaper print with it. It didn't help me. I wasn't any world-beater before and I was a little less after.

BK: Glenn Wright was the shortstop when you were with the Dodgers.

CS: Glenn had had a little arm trouble before he came to Brooklyn. When he was in Pittsburgh, he and that [Pie] Traynor . . . you couldn't get a base hit on the left side of that infield. Nothin' went through. And Wright could go in the hole and throw you out. Traynor, also, had great range and a fine arm.

Glenn Wright's arm wasn't quite so good by the time he got over to Brooklyn, but it was adequate. And he could still hit.

BK: Speaking of hitters, how about Lefty O'Doul?

CS: Oh, that was the smartest hitter of 'em all. (Laughs) He had the misfortune to come up with arm trouble. He knew he could run so he just studied that hitting and he became a real hitter. I mean, he was a real smart hitter. And a fine fella.

BK: You had some pretty good pitchers in Brooklyn, too: Van Lingle Mungo, Dutch Leonard, Boom Boom Beck, Dazzy Vance, Ray Benge.

CS: Sloppy Thurston, [Fred] Heimach. Those were good pitchers but when you stop to think of it, at that time you could take the Cubs. They had [Charlie] Root, [Guy] Bush, [Sheriff] Blake, [Pat] Malone. And all the clubs had three or four real good pitchers. Those boys that we had in Brooklyn were good pitchers but most clubs had a bunch of good, hard throwers. Max Carey was the manager when I went over there in '32 and then Casey Stengel took over.

BK: How was Stengel?

CS: (Laughs) Oh, he was Stengel. Never a dull moment.

BK: Frenchy Bordagaray was another of your Brooklyn teammates.

CS: He was a bit of a character but a likable one. It seemed like he'd get in a little slump and they'd take him out of the lineup and when he went back in he'd wear 'em out for a week. Then he'd tail off. (Laughs) That seemed to be the history of the fella. Good hitter.

BK: After a few years with the Dodgers you went back to the minors. In 1935 you were on the suspended list.

CS: I went to the minor leagues managing the farm clubs for Brooklyn. In '35 I stayed out and played semipro ball up here in Maine.

BK: You managed for several years and then went back to Brooklyn as a coach.

CS: I was in the Bi-State League in '36, the 3-I League in '37, the Eastern League in '38 and '39, and with Montreal in '40, '41, and '42.

BK: Did you want to become a major league manager?

CS: No. That wasn't my ambition at all. I never really prepared myself for that. I just had no ambition in that direction.

BK: In 1945 at the age of 43 you caught a few games for Brooklyn.

CS: We were hurtin' for catching and I'd been active, you know, and my arm was good and my health was good and I caught a few games for 'em. We finally picked up Johnny Peacock from the Red Sox and then I went back to my scoutin'.

BK: You were credited with being the first to scout Jackie Robinson.

CS: No, I never claimed I scouted Jackie Robinson. I brought him in.

Mr. Rickey sent me to Chicago. He called me in one day and he said, "I want you to go to Chicago Friday and see a game between the Kansas City Monarchs and the Chicago Lincoln Giants, paying particular attention to a shortstop named Robinson. And I want you to pay particular attention to his arm. I want you to identify yourself."

Up to this time, we'd been scoutin' the colored league and nobody told us to, but we'd made ourself as inconspicuous as possible. But he said, "Introduce yourself. Tell him who sent you and what you want to see."

Well, I did. I got to Chicago and I went down to the front box and when Robinson came out, I called him over and told him what my errand was. He couldn't imagine why it would be that. He asked a half a dozen times, "Why is Mr. Rickey interested in my arm?" I said, "Well, that's a good question, but I can't answer it. I have ideas."

You know, we had a club in Brooklyn, a Negro club. I guess they were the Brown Bombers. A lot of people thought we were scoutin' for that club, but when Rickey told me, "If you like this boy's arm, bring him in if his schedule will permit. If not, make an appointment for me and I will come out there." Now I know we're not scoutin' for the Brown Bombers and I know he knows an awful lot about this boy. I knew he did that, anyway, because I knew Wendall Smith, a colored newspaper writer for one of the Pittsburgh papers, a colored paper, and I talked to quite a few people and I knew that they had furnished Rickey information on all the colored players.

So, I thought, if this boy is *that* good, why is his arm so entirely important? I mean, if he's that good, there's other places he can play if he, by any chance, doesn't have a super arm.

I don't know how good Robinson's arm was. I mean, I never saw him throw from the shortstop position. I saw him play first base and second base and that's all I ever saw him play. But I would guess that it was an adequate shortstop's arm.

We were hurtin' for infielders at that time. It was 1945 when we were scoutin' the Negro National League and when we signed him we put him up to Montreal [in '46] for a year.

BK: When he came to Brooklyn in '47, you became his first major league manager.

CS: Yep. I managed the first two games of the season. We played Boston in Brooklyn.

BK: And retired undefeated.

CS: That's right. (Laughs) Quite a record.

BK: Durocher had already moved Robinson to first base.

CS: Oh, yeah. Robinson had worked at first base in spring training somewhat. When we came back from the south, [George] Sisler worked with him a little bit and he played that first base like he was born there.

BK: He was an amazing athlete.

CS: Oh, you can say that again.

BK: How was his reception those first two games in Brooklyn?

CS: It was just another game to him. I mean, he took the beatin' in '46 in the International League. That's where he took the beatin'. I mean, professional ball was just another game, another day. (Laughs)

You know, in '46 Jacksonville cancelled an exhibition game; Deland, Florida, cancelled an exhibition game. That hurt him terribly. He thought he was deprivin' the players; he thought he was the means of the games bein' cancelled and some boy was bein' deprived of an opportunity to make the club. It hurt him.

BK: Was there much of a problem in Montreal?

CS: Oh, no. None whatsoever. Montreal is just like Cuba, I would say—no segregation at all.

BK: Let's get back to your career for a minute. You hit two home runs. Do you remember them?

CS: (Laughs) You don't have to have much of a brain to remember two. It's not like I was Babe Ruth and had all those to remember.

Like I told you before, I was an orthodox hitter to start with and I hit .368 in the New England League [1926]. But when I'd get to hit once a week [in Cincinnati], I'd hit a ball fairly good but I got tired of seein' that battin' average at a hundred-and-forty or a hundred-and-fifty. And that went on for two years. So I had to become more of a line drive hitter and I took a big heavy bat and choked up on it and, like I said, I legged a few. I could run. I knew I could do that, 'cause I'd outrun a few guys.

I hit one [home run] in Brooklyn and one in Philadelphia. The first one I think I hit against Doug McWeeny [1929] and the second one [1930] I hit off a fellow I know, lives around Boston, but I can't recall his name now.

BK: You saw major league ballplayers over 40 years. Who was the best one?

CS: That's a tough question. Best all-around player, most valuable all-around player? I would have to go with Willie Mays. I think he had more ways of beatin' you than anybody and he used them. He could do everything; he had it all.

BK: Who was the best pitcher?

CS: There were so many good ones back in those days. I'd have to study that for a while.

They have some good pitchers now. I'm not like a lot of ancient guys, thinkin' things were best in my day, and I think baseball probably overall is better now than it was then. They play the fundamentals better. I think the managing and coachin's better. You can go to a high school game now and you can see every kid slides properly and the pitcher knows how to pitch, I mean, to stand on the rubber and all.

But the arms have deteriorated. This TV, which brought in all the money, destroyed the arms. My wife has a couple of nephews right here in Waldoboro; they played Little League ball. They'd play Tuesday night and dash home and watch TV. They all had their favorite programs and then they'd play a game Friday night.

Go back in the so-called good old days, we threw the ball seven days a week. From a little old country town, if we didn't play [a game] we'd pitch to each other. We played ball every day, seven days a week. Good arms were a dime a dozen, and they were, up until—well, after the war the kids had more to do. There was a wave of prosperity. A lot of kids were able to buy a second-hand car and, course, that kept 'em away from baseball. (Laughs) We didn't have those temptations.

When you use it [the arm] in those tender years, that's when you develop it, I think. And they didn't have the disabled list back in those days. (Laughs) I think those were better arms physically, not that possibly the guys throw just as hard now—maybe some of 'em throw harder—but, overall, they had better arms back in those days, less arm trouble.

BK: What was your biggest thrill in baseball?

CS: Oh, I don't know. I caught an opening game in Cincinnati in '27, '28—somewhere along there. I don't know what happened to the other catcher but I guess that was the most exciting thing at that point.

BK: Tell us about Roberto Clemente.

CS: Mr. Rickey sent me to Richmond to see Joe Black pitch, when they sent Joe Black to Montreal, and they were playin' a five-game series in Richmond. He said, "Get down there and see him pitch." Well, I got down there and Joe Black hasn't pitched yet. (Laughs)

They had this baby-faced Negro in right field. They were having their infield and outfield practice and here was this kid out there—real great arm. You couldn't help noticin' that. He wasn't playin', though.

Max Macon was the manager and Max had played for me in Montreal. 'Long about the seventh inning they're behind and they have a lefthand pitcher out there and who should go up to pinch-hit? This boy in right field. I didn't even know what his name was then; I didn't have any battin' order.

He hit a routine ground ball at the shortstop and the play at first base was just bang-bang. I mean, they just did get him. So he's showed me he could throw and run right then.

The next four nights I was out there watchin' him in battin' practice and his form was a little bit unorthodox but he had a good power stroke. I mean, he was a pretty good-lookin' hitter and you can't miss that kind of talent.

So I wrote Mr. Rickey. I said, "Joe Black hasn't pitched but I have you a draft choice." We were finishin' last by a big margin and the National League had first draft. And I told Macon when I left there, "Take good care of our boy, Max. Don't let him get in trouble. Treat him like you would your own son." (Laughs)

"Oh, you don't want him!" (Laughs)

I said, "Max, we've been friends for quite a while but don't give me that."

We had our draft meetin' and one of the scouts had a candidate—an infielder in the Southern League—and another one had a pitcher someplace else and Mr. Rickey said, "Do you have a candidate, Clyde?" and I said, "Yeah. Clemente with Montreal."

"Any of the rest of you fellas seen Clemente?"

One fella said, "I did. I didn't like him."

"What didn't you like?"

"Well," he said, "he wasn't playin' for one thing and I didn't like his arm." (Laughs)

I didn't say anything. I didn't want to embarrass the guy but I knew very well he didn't get a look at the arm. The boy may have been poutin' or something because he wasn't playin'. I told him afterwards, "You didn't see his arm. He probably just didn't feel like throwin' but don't think he can't throw."

Well, you've got one guy that says he's got a great arm, another guy doesn't like it. First choice is *very* important to us, so he [Rickey] sent

George Sisler and Holly Hague to Montreal to see him. Naturally, we drafted him. For $4,000 it wasn't a bad deal.

BK: You spent a lifetime in baseball. Any regrets?

CS: Oh, no. I wasn't any genius in school and I didn't have any high ambitions. I wanted to play ball—that's all I wanted to do. I wasn't big enough to be too good but I thought what there was of me was pretty good.

BK: Would you do it all again?

CS: Oh, yeah! But never look back. You meet a lot of nice people and you see a lot of real estate. (Laughs) I've been in every state in the union and most of the ballparks, Mexico, Cuba, Puerto Rico, Dominican Republic, good part of Canada. In a good part of my career I was single and you enjoy travellin' and goin' to new places when you're at that age.

Clyde LeRoy (Sukey) Sukeforth

Born November 30, 1901, Washington, ME
Ht. 5′10″ Wt. 155 Batted Left and Threw Right

Year	Team	G	AB	R	H	2B	3B	HR	RBI	SB	BA	SA
1926	CinN	1	1	0	0	0	0	0	0	0	.000	.000
1927		38	58	12	11	2	0	0	2	2	.190	.224
1928		33	53	5	7	2	1	0	3	0	.132	.208
1929		84	237	31	84	16	2	1	33	8	.354	.451
1930		94	296	30	84	9	3	1	19	1	.284	.345
1931		112	351	22	90	15	4	0	25	0	.256	.322
1932	BrkN	59	111	14	26	4	4	0	12	1	.234	.342
1933		20	36	1	2	0	0	0	0	0	.056	.056
1934		27	43	5	7	1	0	0	1	0	.163	.186
1945		18	51	2	15	1	0	0	1	0	.294	.314
10 years		486	1237	122	326	50	14	2	96	12	.264	.331

RAY HAYWORTH

50-Year Man

1926–1945

Defensive ace Ray Hayworth had been his team's number one catcher for four seasons and during that time the club's fortunes had risen from a

***Above:* Ray Hayworth (George Brace photo).**

near-cellar finish to the middle of the pack. A solid nucleus was there and a fine young pitching staff had been assembled. It looked as if the team would be in contention in the coming season.

A couple of important deals were made. One was a trade of .300-hitting oufielders but the man Hayworth's team received was a superstar destined for the Hall of Fame while the one given up was merely a very good hitter. In the other deal the team gave up a minor league catcher and cash for the best backstop in the game, maybe the best in baseball history. And he was named the new manager as well. With the team on the verge of a pennant, Ray Hayworth was suddenly the number two catcher.

Hayworth would have been the starter on at least half of the teams in the league and he knew it. It would have been easy to be bitter. Instead, he played the best baseball he could and helped the team in every way he could, even though his playing time was limited. The results were his two finest seasons offensively, and the new catcher-manager guided the team to two league titles and a World Championship.

The principles in the above deals were, respectively, Goose Goslin, John Stone, Johnny Pasek, $100,000, and Mickey Cochrane. The team was the 1934 Detroit Tigers.

Ray Hayworth spent a half-century in baseball. After his playing days he climbed from the scouting ranks, where he was recognized as one of the best, to the front office. He's over 90 now and has long since retired, but he has an uncanny memory. He recalls things that happened over 60 years ago as well as he remembers what went on last week.

* * *

BK: You're in your 90s now.

RAY HAYWORTH: That's gettin' pretty well along, I think. I saw a piece in *The Sporting News* where Rick Ferrell is the oldest living member of the Hall of Fame. Charlie Gehringer was the oldest and he passed away a short time ago. Rick is 89; he's a little over a year younger than I am. He's born in '05 and I was born in '04, so we're right there together—kind of grew up together here, played against each other for ten years in the American League, so we've been friendly enemies all these years.

He's great. Just one of the best. He's a remarkable fella and I always enjoyed goin' into Detroit after I was in the scouting and director of player personnel. I always managed to get up to the office and visit with Rick because he spent so many years there in Detroit with [Jim] Campbell.

He's not very active with them anymore. He lives up there in Troy,

Michigan, right close to where Charlie Gehringer's home was. He was a very nice fella. I always enjoyed visiting with him.

BK: Billy Rogell and Chief Hogsett are in their 90s, too.

RH: Yeah, we're all right there together. They and Gehringer and I—there were five of us—all of us within less than a year apart. There's five of us left—Flea Clifton and [Elden] Auker and of course Chief and [Rogell] and that brings us up to five and that's all that's left of the '35 Tigers.

Great team! Just great! We had four guys off of there that made the Hall of Fame.

BK: And maybe another one who should have—Tommy Bridges.

RH: I think so. I've always felt very strongly that Bridges should've been in. Unfortunately, he passed away quite a number of years ago with cancer but I think if he had lived he probably would've made it.

BK: Mickey Cochrane liked to catch fastballs, so when Bridges pitched you were his catcher.

RH: Yeah, I caught Bridges. Bridges and I worked together for many years. I was in Detroit when he came along, you know. An interesting thing about Bridges—the first day he joined the club we were playin' a series in Yankee Stadium and we got in trouble there in the early innings so they just brought Bridges out of the bullpen to pitch to Babe Ruth.

Well I thought, what a way to break into the American League! He got a strike on Babe and he threw him two of those *sharp* curves and the Babe turned around and walked back to the bench. He'd never seen one quite that sharp. I'll tell you, he'd start it at the point of your shoulder and I'd catch it in the dirt.

BK: Everyone who saw him says no one ever threw one better.

RH: Yeah. He and Mace Brown had two of the best curveballs I ever saw. They were just like fallin' off a table.

Mace lives right near me here. Mace is a great guy. I played golf with him—back when we were playin' golf—for many, many years and he's the only fella I ever saw in my whole life (laughs)—he flubbed a ball one day when we were playin' up at Richmond—we were up there on a scouting trip—he flubbed this ball and it was the first time I ever remember seein' a human bein' tryin' to kick himself. He tried four or five times—he couldn't do it. (Laughs) It was the funniest thing you ever saw. But Mace, he's a good golfer and I always loved to play with him. He and my brother Red—he lives near me—and Gil English—who I played with in Detroit and Brooklyn—we had a great foursome. We played for years and years till, well, I guess I aged out first. I just got to where I couldn't walk and I had a heart condition develop when I had my prostate removed and I've been wearin' a pacemaker for ten years and it's just been wonderful, just great.

I don't do anything much anymore. My heart doctor said to take it easy, don't dig any ditches. (Laughs) This pacemaker has been a life-saver for *so* many people. I never knew so many had 'em till I got one. They're just wonderful.

We've got quite a few old-time ballplayers around here that's still alive and kickin'. When I grew up along with the Ferrells and Sam Gibson and all that bunch—Cliff Bolton and all—we could've gotten a major league club out of this county I live in. Man, everybody here—all the kids from my age up—played nothin' but baseball all their life, started out as kids and just kept on playin'. We played from kids through school and on into grade and high school and then into prep school. I went to Oak Ridge Military prep school here at Oak Ridge, North Carolina, and we had one of the greatest coaches there I think I ever knew of. My brother Red was the *ninth* player he sent out of that prep school to the major leagues. When Red went up to St. Louis in '44, he said, "I'm happy now. That's the ninth player I've sent out of here to the major leagues." Colonel Holt was his name.

He was Wes Ferrell's coach, too. Wes went to school over there. There's another fella I think should be in the Hall of Fame. He was great. He was just one of the greatest competitors I ever saw in the field. He just battled you right down to the last inch. I swear sometimes I think he'd rather give you a base on balls than give you a ball you can hit. (Laughs) He'd draw that line fine. He had a *great* career.

BK: His early death, too, is probably what's holding him back.

RH: That's absolutely right.

BK: But they finally elected Arky Vaughan and he died young, so maybe there's still a chance for guys like Bridges and Ferrell.

RH: There could be. They've got a chance to still get in there but it takes some doin'. Somebody's got to push and after a fella's dead and gone for 20, 25 years everybody has a tendency to forget.

BK: You signed out of prep school?

RH: Yeah. I signed with Detroit my third year at Oak Ridge. That was in 1925 and in 1926 I went to spring training with Detroit and Toronto was their Triple-A club at that time and I went on up to Toronto and opened the season. I played two or three games and Johnny Bassler broke his leg in Detroit so they called me into Detroit and I went over there and stayed from May, I guess it was, until along the latter part of August and I caught some games and I got along very well for a rookie.

Ty Cobb was the manager at that time. What an experience for me! I had heard about Walter Johnson and Tris Speaker and Eddie Collins and all those fellas for so many years, from a kid up, and I had to pinch myself when I was out there competing against 'em.

I remember I hit against Walter Johnson one day in Washington. I went to the ballpark and Cobb says, "You're the catcher today," and that scared me to death. (Laughs) I caught the game and hit against Johnson and that was the thrill of a lifetime to me, just to get in the ballgame and hit against him. It got up to the seventh inning with the game at stake, and who do you think pinch-hit for me? Ty Cobb! And he doubled off of Johnson to left-center and broke the game open right there. I thought, well, what a day I had to get to the major leagues in '26, the opportunity to hit against Walter Johnson and play against so many great playes at that point in time just finishing their careers. I hit a couple balls off of him, one to left field and one to shortstop and, course, then he couldn't throw as hard as he used to.

I'll tell you something interestin' about Walter Johnson. One day Whitlow Wyatt and I were in Detroit out on the bench and, course the visiting club would come by our dugout going on the field in Detroit and Walter stopped for a visit with us for a few minutes. We said, "Walter, we've always heard—we know you've been such a great pitcher, we'd just like for you to tell us how *hard* could you throw?" And he said, "I'll just be honest with you, boys. I could throw just as *hard* as I wanted to." (Laughs) I believed it 'cause we always said after he had retired from active duty in Washington, he'd go out and pitch battin' practice and we'd sit there and watch him and say, "Heck, he can throw harder'n anybody on his staff now!" You know what he reminded me of? You ever watch fellas—you probably have, you've been around horses—that can pop that blacksnake whip? That's just the way his arm impressed me—just like crackin' a whip! Boy, could he ever throw that ball! Course back then, the balls we played with were rough and I swear you could hear 'em hum.

You know, back in those days it's remarkable—I know Nolan Ryan did some remarkable things—you remember one time I believe Walter Johnson pitched in the World Series and he pitched about three out of four days in a row. (Laughs) Boy, what an arm! How could you do it? But he did.

The whole pitching picture's changed since our day. I remember when I first went to Detroit and took over as first-string catcher there in 1930 for four years before Cochrane came over, our pitchers just raised sand if they couldn't get to be in there for nine innings. They felt embarrassed if they couldn't stay nine. But now, a fella gets in four or five or six innings, why, they bring on the shock absorbers and then they get to that eighth or ninth and they bring on their stopper. It's changed the whole style of playing.

And with the designated hitter. I have never been too keen for that but that's just one opinion. (Laughs) The most fortunate people in the world are the designated hitters. The old guy's broke down; all he can do's swing the bat. I'll tell you, you take all those great hitters, if they can drag themselves up to the plate they could always hit. It's remarkable how they can swing that bat—timing and coordination and everything. It's like Jimmy Dykes said one time, "Nature gives you so much in your wrists and he gave just a few of 'em a lot more than anybody else." I used to stand back of the plate and watch Hank Aaron hit in spring training when I was with the Braves there for a long time. I'd just stand there and watch the quickness in his bat. You just can't imagine how quick! And the same way with Ernie Banks. The wrists they had, and the quickness! Course Ruth had it and Willie Mays and the great hitters had it, but so many of us, instead of dealing out a lot of that we just got a little mediocre chunk of it. (Laughs)

So there you are—you hit .265 and .280 and .290 and .300, but these guys—I looked here the other day at a calendar I had; I just couldn't believe the figgers [*sic*] I was readin' hardly. Ty Cobb had a lifetime batting average, I think, of .367 for 23 years! Can you imagine that?

Ty Cobb, when I was up there in '26, he was very friendly with me and one day I was talkin' to him. He'd come out and hit about eight or nine in a row and change his feet around and hit some to left, some to center, and some to right. One day he looked out at me and he said, "Hey, kid." He said, "You know, this hitting is just a simple twist of the wrist." (Laughs) I always told people I don't know whether I ever got that little simple twist or not. (Laughs) I'm afraid I didn't get too much of it.

Boy, what a hitter! What concentration! You know, these fellas—Williams and all—it's *amazing* all the physical ability and their ability to *concentrate*—just absolutely shut the world out when they went up there to the plate and deciding what pitch to hit. Gehringer was right much that way. Gehringer was the best two-strike hitter I ever saw. He'd be up there and the first two pitches—two strikes—and he'd wind up hittin' a line drive to left-center or right-center. He was a remarkably good hitter.

They've gotta have good eyesight. Course, the fellas that have the quick wrists, they can look at a ball a little longer and still hit it out in front. The rest of us ordinary guys, we'd have to hit it out in front or it'd jam you. There's a difference there. I can see it in catchin' so many years and watchin' hitters and all, why, you get a pretty good perspective of what a fella can do up there with a bat in his hands. Very observing people they were. They could figure out the pitchers and his out pitches and his second and third rate pitches they just lived off of 'em and they could do it.

BK: You set a record for catchers—439 consecutive errorless chances.

RH: I started that streak in '31 and I went a year. I caught a hundred games, went 439 chances without an error. And we were playin' in Philadelphia and I was workin' the game with Earl Whitehill and I think it was about the seventh or eighth inning they got a couple men on base. I called for a curveball and, course, he had a *good* one, and he threw a fastball high and tight. Course, everybody would've missed it. I did and the man on third base scored and they had to give me an error.

In checkin' with Rogell at shortstop and Gehringer at second base, both of 'em verified my call for a curveball and Whitehill just misread my sign. Course he came in the clubhouse and said, "I sure hate that I broke your string." He said, "It's just one of those things that I just misread the sign." Course, you know when you call for a curveball and you expect a good one and they throw a high, hard one, you aren't gonna touch it. That's how I broke my record. I think I might've gone to 500.

The record ahead of me was Johnny Bassler in Detroit and he was holding it at 285 chances. Gosh, I went to 439. It was unfortunate the way it happened but I guess it had to happen sometime. You know, I was most fortunate with the gloves we used then and the equipment and all to have gone that long without an error.

I've got my three gloves, one that I used in that streak, here at the house and I've got two more, another one I used in the American League and then I've got the one I used in the National League over at Brooklyn. I got 'em here in my memorabilia corner and the last pair of shoes I wore.

My wife was a great saver of write-ups and pictures and World Series mementos that we got and all and she kept 'em all. The '34 and '35 Series, she kept all the World Series programs, both Detroit and St. Louis and Chicago, and I have those back here on a board and I've got the '35 program and all the players in there—their pictures—and all of 'em are autographed by the players. A fella offered me $750 for that thing. (Laughs) I wouldn't sell it.

I've got so *many* things—write-ups, I've got a wonderful collection of pictures, autographed balls. I've got a ball here that Babe Ruth autographed for me in 1931 in the clubhouse in Detroit and it's just perfect—the signature and everything—and I've kept it in a good dry place and it's just in mint condition. I've got the '35 World Series ball autographed, and '34 and '29 and '30. I think I've got ten or eleven autographed balls here and I've got my model bat from Hillerich and Bradsby.

I had a real good model they made for me and at the time they gave me a set of Grand Slam golf clubs for the right to use my signature on the bat. You know, my older son still has that set of clubs today but they're antiques and he's got 'em up on the wall over at his home. When I signed with 'em, they not only gave me the set of clubs, they gave me a golf bag to go with it.

Last year—my grandchildren have grown up now and my great-

Ray Hayworth (courtesy National Pastime).

grandchildren are comin' on—my grandchildren finally realized, when they got up 20 years old and beyond, that I played major league baseball. They said, "Well, Papaw, don't you have a model bat?" And I said, "No, but I'll write Hillerich and Bradsby and see if they still have the stats on mine." So I did. Darned if they didn't send me four of my model bats just exactly like I had. And then it was gonna take eight to go around so I had to send back and get four more. (Laughs) I was surprised because I hadn't played an inning since 1945 in Brooklyn. They still had my bat—the weight, length, and everything. I saved one—I've got one here I'm keeping for my own memorabilia corner.

I used about a 33 length and 33–34 ounce, mostly 33 ounce. I had to use a little lighter bat. I've got Greenberg's bat back here. Gosh, I pick that thing up and feel of it, I say, "How in the world could he hit 58 home runs one year with that bat?" I could hardly swing it it was so big and heavy. [He was] big and powerful—great hitter. He should've broken that record that year; that last weekend he just sorta froze up and went in a slump or he would've broken it. We went into Cleveland for a series and he had a good chance to break it there but he didn't hit a home run the whole series at the end of the season. We felt sorry for him but that's just the way it went. He was a tremendous hitter. Boy, I tell you, he could hit that curveball! If he got it a little bit inside it was good-bye over the left field fence.

One time we went up to Grand Rapids, Michigan, there at the Kellogg's place and played an exhibition game. The owner up there, one of the big wheels at Kellogg's, said, "Nobody's ever hit a ball over the center field fence here," and he said, "If any of you fellas do it, we'll give you the Kellogg factory." (Laughs) Greenberg went up and hit one *way* over the center field fence and he didn't get the factory. (Laughs) I've seen him hit 'em out of the park everywhere. He had great power and a great man with it—just a very impressive gentleman over the years we knew him.

BK: When Cochrane came over, you had been the first-string catcher there for the better part of four years.

RH: Yes, I was, and I got along real good but I knew when Mick came over that he was a playin' manager and was at the peak of his career and he was gonna do most of the catchin'. I said right off the bat, I told my wife, I said, "I'd rather be here second-string catcher than be in St. Louis Browns on a last-place club."

Both of us benefited because of him bein' a lefthand hitter, he hit against all those tough righthanders that I used to battle and the lefthanders that *he* used to battle I hit against those and, as a result, both of us hit better than we ever did before. I hit .293 in '34 and .309 in '35 and Cochrane's batting averages, which the records show, were real good. I didn't have to hit against the tough righthanders and he didn't have to hit against the tough lefthanders. I accepted it and was just glad to be there with a championship club.

I have a book here where they made a survey of all the catchers in Detroit for the last 99 years and I made the first team as a defensive catcher.

There's been an awful lot of good catchers go through Detroit all that time so I felt mighty proud to be selected as the all-time defensive catcher. Mother Nature gave me a wonderful arm—I could really throw and throw accurately. I threw out Ben Chapman three times in one game in New York one day in the Yankee Stadium and the son of a gun was the league-leading base stealer at that time. (Laughs) I nailed him three times, *twice* tryin' to steal third base. He always tried to get me—he was a tough ballplayer.

BK: The Tigers were favored in the 1934 World Series.

RH: We felt very confident when we went from St. Louis back to Detroit that we would win it. We had 'em down, 3 to 2, and the Deans beat us a game apiece and beat us out of it, but the next year we beat the Cubs in six games with a *great* Series, every game 2 to 1, 1 to nothin' except the second game when we knocked Root out. But it was a great Series. Every day I'd look up and it'd be the sixth or seventh inning and you'd wonder how in the heck you'd played that many innings that quick.

The Cardinals Series was an *outstanding* Series. Those Deans were just invincible and we had great pitching and had some great baseball played in those two Series. As I look back over my years in baseball, I just don't think that it could have been any better.

Very little difference in the teams ['34 and '35]. *Very* little difference. The club held on. See, we finished first in '34 and '35 and second in '36 and '37 and fourth in '38, so we had a good club riding through there for four or five years.

Come on down to '38 and Birdie Tebbetts was coming on strong then, so they sold me to the Brooklyn club and I went over there and was there in '38 and '39. Down toward the end of the season I was traded to the Giants for Jimmy Ripple. I was with the Giants in '39 and all of '40 and then I went to St. Louis Browns in '42 and [at] cuttin' down time they released me. I was a ten-year man and I signed with the Cardinals and I stayed with the Cardinals a while and unfortunately they won the pennant and World Series that year but I was gettin' along near the end of my career and Mr. Rickey came to me one day and he said, "We're gonna change managers over in Rochester and we want you to go over there as playin' manager. It'll be a great experience for you." I was happy for the opportunity and I went over there and managed the club for the rest of the year and then Mr. Rickey went from St. Louis to Brooklyn that winter and he took me with him. I was there with Brooklyn in '43, '44, and '45 and I was on the active list in '44 and '45. I finished my career there. I was a coach mainly in '43; in '44 and '45 I played a few games—available on the active list—but I couldn't catch much anymore. I was gettin' too old. (Laughs)

I was very fortunate. Mr. Rickey started me in scouting the last couple years with George Sisler and Wid Matthews. We covered all the colored leagues in New York. Every Sunday we'd see a doubleheader at the Yankee Stadium or Polo Grounds, whichever club was out of town, and we'd get to see a doubleheader and get to see four teams. We had the dope on *all* those colored players; that's the reason Mr. Rickey went out and cornered the market on 'em. I did the special assignment on Buck Leonard and all those fellas. We saw most all of the good ones.

I also had the special assignment when I later went from Brooklyn to the Cubs. I was there nine years as special assignment scout and scouting director. I personally signed Ernie Banks and we arranged and bought him from the Kansas City Monarchs. Course, he's a Hall of Famer. He was one of the best finds I ever made.

How we got a tip on him — they played an exhibition game down with our farm club at Macon, Georgia, in that South Atlantic League and Tom Gordon, the business manager, called us the next day and he says, talkin' to Wid Matthews, "Wid, there's a young colored shortstop on that club you had better take a quick look at." He said, "Other scouts are startin' to look at him and he looks great."

So they called me and I flew out to Davenport, Iowa, and met the club and I watched him play there and back in Kansas City and on into Chicago and, gosh, I'd never seen a young player look better than he did. I told Wid Matthews — he was our general manager and he came out to White Sox park — and I said, "We'd better make a deal *quick* on this fella or we're gonna lose him."

So I made an appointment for him that night with Tom Beard, the owner of the [Kansas City] club — an appointment at Wrigley Field the next morning. He brought Banks out there. They sat right there and made a deal. What do you think we bought Banks for from Kansas City Monarchs? $23,000. (Laughs) Two or three years later, Mr. Busch came over there and he was talkin' to Mr. Wrigley and he says, "I'll tell you what I'll do. I'll give you 500,000 for Banks." Mr. Wrigley says, "500,000," he says, "I don't want 500,000. I just want another Banks." (Laughs)

His contract was bought outright from Kansas City; they owned the rights to him. That's the way you dealt in those days with the colored teams.

I had a good chance to get a great start in scouting through Mr. Rickey and scouting the colored clubs. I went on into Chicago and I was there 13 years, then I went to Milwaukee and Atlanta for another nine years and my last three years I went with John McHale up to Montreal. I retired in '73, so I had a good long career.

The last big players that I scouted — there was a couple of 'em in Montreal where I went out to California. I scouted [Gary] Carter; I saw him play in high school out there. Gosh, what an athlete he was and we were able to get to him in the draft and we got him and signed him. Course, he's a Hall of Famer, or will be. He was just a great, great catcher. And I scouted [Steve] Rogers, too, the righthander. He was a great pitcher—had a short career, hurt his arm—but he was a top-flight pitcher.

All along the line we signed some good ones—great careers and all of 'em don't make good, you know. A lot of 'em didn't do so well. It was a great experience for me to be in the scouting field and I was director of player personnel for John McHale in Milwaukee and helped a great deal in the front end of the thing there. Everything I've been into as a player and scout and director of scouting, it made up a wonderful career for me and I was just fortunate along the way to be with good clubs and good players.

BK: Duke Snider.

RH: I was managing the Fort Worth club in '46 for Brooklyn. We had a great young club and Mr. Rickey called, he said, "We got a young player that played young and he's been in the Navy and we wanna send him down to you." So they sent him down and it was Duke Snider.

I started playin' him and, good night, he knocked all the fences down but he never had hit against lefthand pitching. We were down in San Antone [*sic*] one night and my other outfielder got hurt. I said, "Duke, this is the night you're breakin' in against a lefthander." (Laughs) He liked to had a fit. And he hit against [Hooks] Iott, which was the strikeout king of the league that year. He just said he just felt awkward. I said, "Now, Duke, you're gonna play major league and you're gonna have to learn to hit lefthanders. Just might as well start." And from then on the rest of the season I never did take him out of a game when a lefthander pitched. I let him hit against *all* the lefthanders. By the time that season was over, he was startin' to wear *them* out. He was a great young kid and what great talent he had. He had a wonderful career and he *rightfully* belongs in the Hall of Fame.

BK: Who was the best player you saw?

RH: Well, it's hard. I can name a half dozen. You could sit here and argue all night and never determine who was the greatest, but I'd have to say Ty Cobb was one of the greatest players I ever saw. Then you come on down and you talk about DiMaggio and Willie Mays and Ted Williams and Bill Dickey and Mickey Cochrane. There's just so many *great* players. I just don't think you can honestly say, "I think this player's the greatest player that ever lived," 'cause there's been so many good ones.

I remember seein' Eddie Collins play and Tris Speaker. Well heavens above, they were great players! I wonder what they would do today if they could call back the years and play some games. It would be a sight to see.

BK: Who was the best pitcher?

RH: I could very quickly say it was Bob Feller. That son of a gun, I hated to hit against him. The reason I hated to hit against him so much, he was so great and had so much deception but I said the son of a gun wouldn't look at me at the plate. About the time he released the ball he was lookin' out in right field. (Laughs) I said, "I got a family—a wife and two kids. I can't stay up here at this plate and get killed!" (Laughs) I tell you, I was a dead pull hitter and I hit him just inside the first base line. That's how much difference there was. Oh, his deception—you can't imagine till you put a bat in your hand and go up to the plate to hit against the guy. I've seen him off and on through the years since our playin' days ended and he calls me "Old Folks." (Laughs) He's about to catch up with me now, I believe.

BK: Is there one game that stands out?

RH: I think one of the highlights of my whole baseball career—we were playin' the Yankees in Yankee Stadium. That's when they had Ruth and Gehrig and Dickey and all that bunch in there and we knew that we had to beat them to win the pennant. So we went in there for a crucial series playin' a doubleheader. I caught the first game and Gen Crowder pitched it and we won that game and I got three hits and drove in, let's see, three runs, I believe it was that day against [Lefty] Gomez. I said this has got to be the greatest game I was ever involved in, the most important game, and we won it. Then Schoolboy Rowe went out in the second game and beat 'em, 2 to 1, I think it was. We won that doubleheader that day and broke the Yankees' back and went on and won the pennant. I think that's the greatest day and greatest game I ever played in.

Schoolboy Rowe was a great pitcher. He could really hum that ball. When Schoolboy'd pitch against the Yankees and those top clubs they'd throw ol' Gen Crowder the day before and he'd throw up a lot of junk and screwballs and sinkers and sliders. He'd put the club in a slump. (Laughs) Schoolboy'd come along and shut 'em out. The Yankees swore one time that every time Crowder pitched against 'em it threw 'em into a slump for four or five days. (Laughs) He was really a sharp pitcher. I always liked ol' Gen a great deal. Had a good career.

That Gomez. I hit a home run off him one day in Yankee Stadium and I rounded second base and I can remember very distinctly trottin' towards third and I just thought to myself how many times Ruth made that *same* trot. It was a great feeling. (Laughs) He hit over 600 home runs there and I hit one, but I sure never did forget it. (Laughs)

I was a double hitter. I got a lot of doubles. I didn't have the power to hit the ball out of the park. Along in later years I found out if I'd hit more to right field I'd help the club more and I could hit-and-run and I did that a lot.

Casey Stengel played a very important role in my baseball career. After having a good solid year in 1928 at Shreveport, I went to spring training with the Detroit club and made a very good impression with manager Bucky Harris. However, Bucky felt I had a fault in my hitting I had to overcome to cope with major league pitching. That was to learn to go with pitching up and down the outside of the strike zone to right field; otherwise by being strictly a pull hitter I hit the outside pitches mainly to shortstop and center field. Bucky said, "I want you to go down to the Toledo club where Casey Stengel is the manager. He is a good hitting instructor; have him work with you." Well, Casey did just that. Every day during batting practice he would have the pitchers throw outside with a lot of curveballs. Soon I was going the other way to right field, [and] also hitting behind the runners on hit-and-run plays. As a result, I hit .330 with Toledo and went back and joined Detroit to finish the season and that was the beginning of my 15-plus years in the major leagues. I always felt grateful to Casey for helping me so much.

Casey was a great fellow to play for and I have often said every player should have been exposed to Casey for at least one year. His clubhouse meetings before games were fantastic. I remember one Sunday when the club had fallen into a slump he called a special meeting and began by picking up a fungo bat and striking the top of a trunk a couple times that sounded like a stick of dynamite going off. Then he began by saying, "Have you players been reading the stock market lately?" "Well," he said, "you would be wise to start reading them because the railroad stocks are sure to rise because the way you all are playing a lot of you are gonna be riding the rails in all directions soon."

I remember when we attended the Baseball Writers dinners every year. The toastmaster would always call on Casey for some remarks. Well, Casey would start out on something, then digress all over to whatever came to mind. When the meetings ended, everyone would say, "Wasn't Casey great!" Then they would remark, "Well, what the heck did he say?" (Laughs) Casey Stengel—the one and only!

BK: You had a few interesting oddities along the way in your career.

RH: I changed major league clubs twice without having to leave the ballpark. The first incident came when I was with the Brooklyn club in August 1939. After takin' pregame practice with the Dodgers, I went into the clubhouse to change my shirt when manager Bill Terry came over from the Giants clubhouse and walked straight to my locker and said, "Ray, gather up your gear and come with me. You belong to the Giants now."

Jimmy Ripple came in the deal for me. I immediately went in and put on a uniform and went out to the Giants' dugout. In the third inning, Charlie Dressen, the third base coach for the Dodgers, spotted me on their [the Giants'] bench. Time was called; a big huddle took place to change their signs. (Laughs) Naturally I could read every sign Charlie was giving.

The next change of clubs took place in St. Louis in 1942. I was with the Browns. It was cut-down time—April fifteenth. Being a ten-year player, I was released outright. Branch Rickey, general manager of the Cardinals, knew I was being released and had a catching spot open on their roster. He called me to his office where I signed with them, so all I had to do was take my gear from the Browns' clubhouse over to the Cardinals'. That winter, Mr. Rickey left St. Louis and went to Brooklyn as general manager. He took me with him, where I stayed for the next three years.

Another oddity took place in St. Louis when I was with the Detroit club. We played a doubleheader against the Browns and the most runs were scored in these two games—32—for an all-time record. I remember being walked intentionally two times in one inning by manager Hornsby, who was manager of the Browns at that time.

This game might belong in the "oddity" class. It was called on account of darkness after completing 23 innings. The game took place in Boston on June 26, 1939. The key incident that took place in this game was in the sixteenth inning. Boston had a runner on second base with two out. Manager Casey Stengel sent in a young player to run that could really fly. The next hitter hit a line drive into left field and the game should have ended there, but this kid rounded third base full speed and halfway home fell flat on his face. (Laughs) I took the throw at the plate and ran down to tag him out on the ground. The game then went to the twenty-third inning and was called on account of darkness. This game completed about two months later after I had gone over to the Giants.

BK: Do you receive much fan mail today?

RH: Law, I get more fan mail than I've ever gotten! I declare, this last year I even got a fan letter—a fella sent me some cards for autographs—from Australia! I wrote him a letter and I said, "I've had letters from everywhere in the country but I've never had one from Australia."

I get baseballs and gloves and occasionally a bat and scores of pictures. I've got about eight cards and I got all kinds of cards from all over the country and I sign every one of 'em and send 'em back. I get a big kick out of it.

Interesting thing—I always get letters, you know, and invariably the kid'll say, "My grandfather saw you play," or "My dad saw you play." They tell the kids about it now and they write and get a card and want an autograph. I think as old as I am and as long as it's been since we had the great years in Detroit it's amazing to me how much interest is still in that '34 and '35 Detroit clubs.

BK: Would you do it all again?

RH: Law, yes! I've never known any other life. Actually, I spent 50 years in baseball. The first year I went to Oak Ridge, believe it or not, I went out to West Virginia and played in the Mingo County Coalfield League and that was right in the heart of the country where the Hatfields and McCoys lived and I met some of those people. The only way they could have an umpire out there, they had the sheriff to umpire the games. (Laughs) He'd stand out back of the mound with a big .45 on his hip. I always said he was the worst umpire I ever saw, but it was the only way they could keep order.

The next two years, four or five of us went up and played at Bluefield in the Coalfield League while we were still in school. Vic Sorrell was there with us and some other boys. It was a great experience. I had three years there and then I came on into professional ball and spent all the years up until '73. I decided it was time to retire and I did. And I never regretted it because it was gettin' a little bit hard for me to travel so much and fly so much to look at players—tiring—so I said, what the heck, I'm gonna retire, and I did. I'm glad I did now because I've had some wonderful years since then.

Right now I'm livin' in one of the greatest places in the world—Piedmont Retirement Center. It's a beautiful big place here in Thomasville and the apartments are so nice. Wife and I have got a wonderful apartment here—a two-bedroom apartment. I said I just love it because I can stand right in the middle of the kitchen and reach everything in it. (Laughs) Great people here and I'm only nine miles from over at High Point, my hometown. I have a son livin' there and I have a son that's been in Salisbury for over 20 years, so family's around.

I must be gettin' old. I've got five *great*-grandchildren now.

I don't think I missed many ballparks or many states in the whole country. Every year when I was in the scouting end of this thing, we'd go down to Cuba when we could get in there for years till they shut us out. Castro wouldn't let us come in, but all those years following that we'd go to Puerto Rico and Panama and down to Dominican Republic. We got a lot of good players out of there. They can play—they got good talent.

My brother Red lives right here near me, over in High Point, and caught all the '44 Series in St. Louis. I might tell you this quickly—there were five sons in my family. Four of us played professional baseball and all four of us catchers and Red and I both made the major leagues and we both caught in the World Series. (Laughs) I think that's pretty unusual. Red and

I can only find another brother set and that's Gus Mancuso and his brother [Frank] that both caught in the World Series. I don't know of anybody else.

Raymond Hall Hayworth

Born January 29, 1904, High Point, NC
Ht. 6′ Wt. 180 Batted and Threw Right

Year	Team	G	AB	R	H	2B	3B	HR	RBI	SB	BA	SA
1926	DetA	12	11	1	3	0	0	0	5	0	.273	.273
1929		14	43	5	11	0	0	0	4	0	.256	.256
1930		77	227	24	63	15	4	0	22	0	.278	.379
1931		88	273	28	70	10	3	0	25	0	.256	.315
1932		108	338	41	99	20	2	2	44	1	.293	.382
1933		134	425	37	104	14	3	1	45	0	.245	.299
1934		54	167	29	49	5	2	0	27	0	.293	.347
1935		51	175	22	54	14	2	0	22	0	.309	.411
1936		81	250	31	60	10	0	1	30	0	.240	.292
1937		30	78	9	21	2	0	1	8	0	.269	.333
1938	DetA	8	19	1	4	0	0	0	5	1	.211	.211
	BrkN	5	4	0	0	0	0	0	0	0	.000	.000
1939	BrkN	21	26	0	4	2	0	0	1	0	.154	.231
	NYN	5	13	1	3	0	0	0	0	0	.231	.231
1942	StLA	1	1	0	1	0	0	0	0	0	1.000	1.000
1944	BrkN	7	10	1	0	0	0	0	0	0	.000	.000
1945		2	2	0	0	0	0	0	0	0	.000	.000
15 years		698	2062	221	546	92	16	5	238	2	.265	.332

World Series

Year	Team	G	AB	R	H	2B	3B	HR	RBI	SB	BA	SA
1934	DetA	1	0	0	0	0	0	0	0	0	-	-

OVERTON TREMPER

Dark-Age Dodger

1927–1928

The 1992 Dodgers finished in the cellar for the first time since 1905. For the past 50 years this had been a franchise with an outstanding record but many people do not realize that such was not always the case.

Indeed, even though last place was avoided in each year except 1905, for the first 38 years of this century the Brooklyn Dodgers were a second-division club on 29 occasions. Twenty-nine! There are few people left today who were around to see the Dodgers in those dark days of their history and even fewer who played for them.

One of the oldest living Dodgers of those poor times is Overton

***Above:* Overton Tremper (courtesy Overton Tremper).**

Tremper. A reader may correct me on this, but I think the only man still alive who played for Brooklyn before Overton is Ray Moss.

Tremper was a double anomaly in his day. First, he was college educated. Second, and probably helpful in explaining—at least in part—Brooklyn's woes, he was young and a Dodger at the same time.

Wilbert Robinson evidently did not care for young players. When he took over the reins in 1914, he inherited the youngest team in the National League. By 1918, he had transformed it into the oldest and, with the exception of a couple of years, he kept it there for the rest of his tenure. He preferred to add veterans rather than rookies and one is left to wonder why. The vets did nothing to justify their additions; Uncle Robbie guided the team to 12 second division finishes in his 18 years at the helm.

In 1927, when Overton Tremper joined the team fresh from college at the age of 21, the average Dodger was over 31. Overton's professional career was short but he would do it again.

* * *

BK: You were a Brooklyn boy signed by the Dodgers. Who signed you?

OVERTON TREMPER: The business manager. A fellow named Dave Driscoll came to Penn and scouted me. In those days they didn't have too much on the scouting end of it. He recommended to Robbie [Wilbert Robinson] that I be signed, which I was in June, about the 17th, in 1927. I signed the day I graduated and spent the rest of the year with Brooklyn but didn't get a lot of playing time.

A friend of mine was a good friend of Dave Driscoll and he said there was a fellow down at Penn that could play better than Jigger Statz, who was the center fielder, so they got interested and they followed it up and as a result they signed me. (Laughs) I played about 46 games there in two years.

BK: You only played in 10 games in 1928. Where were you that season?

OT: The spring of '28 they farmed me out to Macon. I went down to Macon and they recalled me the first of August to come back to Brooklyn.

I played professional ball two years. In '29 they sent me back to Macon again and the result was I had a bad year. I hit .286, so they released me. When they released me, that was the beginning of the Depression and I came home and went to work in Brooklyn.

I played semiprofessional ball till 1948 in New York City, where there were mostly ex-big leaguers that came back. They had leagues there like the league up in Cape Cod.

BK: That was a tough level of ball.

OT: Oh, yes. It was good as the Triple-A baseball the minor leagues had. For 20 to 25 years we played all the black teams and that was the nucleus of what the big leagues are now—so many of them are black. We played them all the time—the Homestead Grays, the Pittsburgh Crawfords, and Kansas City Monarchs. Satchel Paige, we played against many, many times.

BK: You were facing better pitching than some in the major leagues at that time.

OT: We faced as good, anyway.

The Negro American and Negro National leagues were in full swing in those days because there wasn't any television and they drew well and the ballplayers that didn't go in the big leagues were playing heavy semipro ball around Boston, Philadelphia, Washington, New York, Pittsburgh, and Kansas City.

The Pittsburgh Crawfords and the Homestead Grays, after the Pirates ended their season, used to play a three-game series and they'd draw 100,000 to the Pirates' stadium.

BK: Some of those teams were probably better than the '92 Dodgers.

OT: (Laughs) I was on some pretty bad Dodger teams, too.

Baseball is much, much better now. They're better trained, they've got better facilities for improving your body and everything. It's far superior to back in the '20s and '30s. From a physical point of view, there's a big improvement and, of course, the gloves have an awful lot to do with it, too.

BK: When you were playing, if you wanted to eat in the winter you had to work. Today, the players don't have to worry about income in the off-season and they can stay fit.

OT: They make so much money now. The poorest player in the big leagues—the lowest paid player—is making probably 25,000 more than Babe Ruth did in his heyday. (Laughs) Go figure that one out.

BK: In those two years with Brooklyn, who was the best player you saw?

OT: Dazzy Vance. I guess the most notorious one was Babe Herman.

Babe Herman was a very eccentric ballplayer. There are a lot of 'em around here now but in those days they weren't quite as eccentric. He was a great hitter—wonderful hitter—poor fielder and a man of his own choosings. He wasn't too well liked by the ballplayers. He was abrasive, you might say egotistical. That might be the nearest thing I can think to describe Babe. Not all the time, naturally, but he was more so than the other players.

BK: Dazzy Vance was a great pitcher.

OT: Remember, in those days there were 25 players and I was the only college ballplayer on the team, so you can understand the background of the other 24. Not that that made any difference, but that was the type of player that came up in those days—came up through the minor leagues into the big leagues and they used to come up when they were 26, 27, 28. In fact, Dazzy Vance never came to Brooklyn from New Orleans until he was close to 30.

Very good man, very *kind* man, very thoughtful, very decent chap. Very, very good pitcher. His battery mate, Hank DeBerry, caught for him down in New Orleans and came up with him as his battery mate because Dazzy wanted Hank there to catch him. He [DeBerry] called himself "the tail end of the kite." (Laughs)

Vance had been there a few years when I arrived and he stayed—guess it was the early '30s before he left.

BK: You mentioned Jigger Statz. He was a legend in the minor leagues.

OT: He was the center fielder there. He was a very nice man. He helped me quite a bit. I was an outfielder and I was very friendly with Jigger. He went back to the coast after he left Brooklyn and played out there for years and years.

He was a great fielder. He couldn't hit. He was like all the little guys—a spray hitter. Jigger was a fine center fielder, at least the two years I watched him play. That's what kept him up there. Brooklyn didn't have much of anything anyway. They were a second division club. In the Pacific Coast League I guess he was a star for years and years.

I guess you could say the best thing I could do was field rather than hit. Hitting is everything in the outfield.

BK: Your first baseman in 1928 was Del Bissonette.

OT: Oh, he was a great ballplayer. He was French. He was a little better than average fielder but a very good hitter. He was one of the few good hitters on the ballclub. He was with Brooklyn five or six years anyway.

BK: His career was shortened by a leg injury.

OT: I didn't follow statistics much. I watch games now and enjoy it but I'm not statistically minded about any of it.

BK: Harvey Hendrick did a lot of pinch-hitting but never seemed to have a position.

OT: Harvey was a great boy. He was just a plain good old hitter. He was a southern boy.

Robbie had mostly all veterans all the time. He'd take cast-off pitchers and bring 'em back and he had a veteran team. They were all old players and they were very nice to me, I would say, outside of Babe Herman, but he wasn't nice to many of 'em anyway, so it didn't matter. Hendrick was fine to me.

He was a *great* hitter. I would say Herman was your best hitter and probably Hendrick was the second best hitter. He was steady. And then Bissonette was the next hitter. But these are vague impressions taken 60 years later. I wouldn't take anything I've said too seriously.

BK: You had a pitcher there for a few years named Jesse Petty.

OT: I was just about to say the second-best pitcher on the club was Jess Petty. He was an old fox; he was old, too—he was in his 30s—and he was a good lefthander. Heavyset man.

And Watty Clark was there. He was a good pitcher, too.

BK: You mentioned that Robinson had veteran players. You were one of the few young players who ever came to the team in those years.

OT: I know. There was a fellow from Holy Cross three or four years before me. Eddie [Doc] Farrell was the captain of Penn before I was and he came up to the Giants and then he was traded to Boston when they brought [Rogers] Hornsby over from St. Louis. There were very, very few college ballplayers. If there were two or three college ballplayers on a team, there were a lot back in the '30s. They didn't get their ballplayers from college.

BK: A lot of them never even finished high school back in those days.

OT: That's quite true. They came up out of sandlots and played minor league ball. They didn't come up [to professional ball] when they were 18 and 19, either; they started when they were 20 to 21.

Like Al Lopez. I roomed with him. He came out of Jacksonville. He came over to Macon the year I came down there in '28—he came up from Jacksonville. He was 19 years old at that time and I was 22 then and I was young but he was a hell of a lot younger—three years younger than I was.

BK: Is there a game that stands out in your career?

OT: Yeah, there's two.

June the 18th, '27—I broke in. I travelled to Cincinnati and broke in as a pinch hitter and got a base hit off Adolf Luque. And then in September, a Sunday before Labor Day in '28, against Boston, we played a doubleheader and I got five hits—a double, a triple, and three singles, which, to me, was an excellent day. Those two days stand out in my mind.

BK: Luque was a good pitcher.

OT: Luque was a good pitcher but at that time he was just about ready to retire. He was past his prime then. He happened to be pitching—I guess he'd been pitching the whole ballgame—and I guess Robbie wanted to see what he bought so he sent me up to hit in the ninth inning. I broke my bat and hit a single up the middle.

BK: Any regrets from your career?

OT: No, I enjoyed every minute of it. If I could have hit. . . . A lot of players that were with me, like Johnny Allen, Dusty Cooke, Ben Chapman, they were all in the same league as I was—they were moved up to Triple-A from where we were in the Sally League and I was sent back, which I don't think was good for me but that's the way they did it. They all went on to play in the big leagues for many years.

I have no regrets; in fact, I owe my whole life to having played baseball. That's all I wanted to do. I didn't like math in high school, so my mother picked the Wharton school. They had accounting but they didn't have regular math, which I hated, but I wound up 25 to 30 years teaching math in high school.

BK: Wharton is a great school. It opens doors anywhere.

OT: I guess it's the best school in the country. It wasn't then, though. I wasn't interested in opening any doors; I was interested in playing baseball, period.

BK: Would you go back and do this again?

OT: Oh, yes! Oh, goodness, yes! Without thinking about it. (Laughs) I might do a few little things differently, knowing where I had failed before through not thinking about my physical well-being.

I caught cold one spring down in spring training coming down on the train from Brooklyn to Clearwater. The first day of practice, the second year I was there, I had to go in a hospital for two weeks. I got a sinus attack or something strange and that ruined me for 1928. When I got well and started playing ball again they brought me back up in August. I would have made sure I wore an overcoat on the train when I went South.

There are little things like that which you look back on you realize were turning points in your career. Anyway, I don't ever look back.

Carlton Overton Tremper

Born March 22, 1906, Brooklyn, NY
Ht. 5'10" Wt. 163 Batted and Threw Right

Year	Team	G	AB	R	H	2B	3B	HR	RBI	SB	BA	SA
1927	BrkN	36	60	4	14	0	0	0	4	0	.233	.233
1928		10	31	1	6	2	1	0	1	0	.194	.323
2 years		46	91	5	20	2	1	0	5	0	.220	.264

RUSS SCARRITT

The Rapid Red Sox Rookie

1929–1932

The triple: no less a hitter than Stan Musial called it "the most exciting play in baseball."

Home runs are often dramatic, but not necessarily exciting. The batter trots leisurely around the bases and no play is made. Most doubles are

Above: **Russ Scarritt (courtesy National Pastime).**

stand-up; frequently the runner coasts into second base, having stopped actually running when he saw the ball skip between the outfielders. But triples are different. On 90 percent or more of three-base hits, there is a play—usually a close one—made at the bag. There is all-out effort by everyone involved: the outfielder and cutoff man have to make quick and accurate throws, the third baseman must receive the throw cleanly and make a rapid tag at a baserunner who is already there, and the runner must run all-out from the second he swings the bat.

Triples are not equal opportunity statistics, however. High triple totals are usually restricted to those players who can motor around the base and have enough strength to get the ball between or over the outfielders. Dave Kingman hit the ball hard and far, but he could not outrun a rock. Maury Wills ran like lightning, but a solid hit for him was a grounder to deep short. Neither of these guys hit many triples.

Triples were a much more prominent part of the game in the dead-ball era. The outfielders played shallow then because very little was hit over them. When a ball was hit hard enough to get through or over, the result was frequently triples. The all-time leaders in career triples and top single-season totals read like a Who's Who of the dead-ball era.

So high triple totals since 1921 have been the exception. Of the 16 original major league franchises, only three—the Yankees, the original Senators/Twins, and the Browns/Orioles—have a post–1920 hitter as the team record holder for triples in a season.

In the live-ball era, Russ Scarritt holds the Boston Red Sox record for triples in a season, with 17 in 1929. That was Scarritt's rookie year; not only did he set the team record that year, he also equalled Charlie Gehringer's league record for rookies in the live-ball era.

Russ Scarritt was the regular left fielder for the Red Sox as a rookie in 1929. It was a bad team, as were all Red Sox teams in those days. (Boston baseball must have been a dreary sight that season with both the city's clubs finishing in the cellar; the Red Sox finished 58-96 and the Braves were 59-98.)

Nevertheless, these were major league ballplayers and Russ Scarritt was the best of the Red Sox that year. He hit .294, with 159 hits, 72 RBIs, and, of course, 17 triples. His numbers were good enough to lead the team in five offensive categories. It was a good rookie year.

Russ was Boston's regular left fielder again in 1930 and, although he again produced well (.289 batting average), his playing time was reduced by about 25 percent. This was partially due to some minor injuries, but primarily because his first wife was dying of cancer and this proved to be a tremendous distraction. "He sort of packed it in," when she passed away, according to his son Jerry.

* * *

BK: How did you begin in professional baseball?

RUSS SCARRITT: I didn't intend to play professional baseball to start with. I was promised an appointment to West Point and when the time came somebody with a little more pull than me got to him [the senator who made the recommendation] and he offered me one for the Coast Guard and I told him to shove it. I didn't want it.

A fella I knew had a chance to manage at Chattanooga and he asked me to go up there with him so I just went. I was 23. I was starting a little late.

BK: Had you played ball in high school and college?

RS: No. I went to prep school—military institute—and the University of Florida, but I didn't play at either place. I just played around in sandlot ball at home.

I played six years in the minors—two years in St. Paul and two years at Greenville in the Sally League and two years at Chattanooga.

BK: When you joined the Red Sox in 1929, you had a great rookie year and were probably the best player on the team.

RS: They were a bad team. I had the most triples of anybody. Seventeen triples was the most of any rookie in the American *or* National League.

BK: Why was your playing time reduced in your second year?

RS: You never know why they don't play you. You're just trading material, I guess. I couldn't understand why they traded me to Washington. I don't know why; I never found out. It just took me off my feet. I just went through the motions, but my heart wasn't in it.

BK: How was Heinie Wagner as a manager?

RS: Heinie Wagner was okay. He was a pretty nice fella. He and Bill Carrigan, both of 'em were nice. Just didn't have anything to work with.

BK: You were fast.

RS: Yeah, I was fast. They didn't let us run a whole lot. I could run more in the minor leagues.

BK: You left the majors in 1932. Did you retire from baseball?

RS: I did. I plugged into oil prospecting out in Texas and dug a few dry holes, and finally gave up on it and had to go to work. Went to work for Ford Motor Company and worked for them for 40 years.

BK: Is there one day in your career that stands out?

RS: Yes. It was a doubleheader we played against Milwaukee the last day of the season [in 1927]. I hit 9 for 10. We were playing in St. Paul and Casey Stengel was managing Toledo against Indianapolis. We had to win both games for him to win the pennant and we did.

BK: Who was the best player you saw?

RS: I think Lou Gehrig was the best I played against. And Babe Ruth.

BK: What about among your teammates?

RS: I guess Earl Webb maybe.

BK: Who was the best pitcher?

RS: Lefty Grove. He was pretty rough on me.

BK: It has been 70 years since you began your career. What do you think of the changes in the game?

RS: I think it's changed for the worse. They don't have to go through the minors like we did. They just throw that money around. It looks like they could give us some of it but they don't do it.

BK: What was your top salary?

RS: 6,000.

BK: Did you save souvenirs from your playing days?

RS: My house burned down on Christmas day right after I quit and burned everything I had saved up. It's all gone.

BK: Do you still receive fan mail?

RS: I receive about three letters a week. Autograph requests.

BK: Do you sign?

RS: Sure I do. There's a club where a band plays every Wednesday night and they introduce me to the customers and I sign autographs. I signed 131 one day out at Wal-Mart. I had to stop for a while and rest.

BK: Do you have any regrets from your baseball days?

RS: No, I really don't. I enjoyed it. I had a good time and I have no regrets about it.

BK: Would you do it again?

RS: Yeah, I'd do it again. Without thinking about it.

Stephen Russell Mallory Scarritt

Born January 14, 1903, Pensacola, FL
Died December 6, 1994, Pensacola, FL
Ht. 5′10½″ Wt. 165 Batted Left and Threw Right

Year	Team	G	AB	R	H	2B	3B	HR	RBI	SB	BA	SA
1929	BosA	151	540	68	159	26	17	1	71	13	.294	.411
1930		113	447	48	129	17	8	2	48	4	.289	.376
1931		10	39	2	6	1	0	0	1	0	.154	.179
1932	PhiN	11	11	0	2	0	0	0	0	0	.182	.182
4 years		285	1037	119	296	44	25	3	120	17	.285	.385

CHIEF HOGSETT

How Do You Spell Relief?

1929–1944

When lefthander Elon "Chief" Hogsett joined the Detroit Tigers in September 1929, the role of the relief pitcher was still in its very early stages. In those days, with a few exceptions, a reliever was either a failed or washed-up starter, a rookie just up, or the number one man on the staff used between starts to hold a lead.

Above: **Chief Hogsett (George Brace photo).**

In Chief's first full season with Detroit—1930—he was the number five man in the rotation, but he relieved as often as he started. In 1931, as the Tigers fought hard to avoid the cellar, seven men started at least 12 games with more or less limited success. Again Chief split his time between the two roles. He also spent time in the minors, with Toronto of the International League.

In 1932 he established his niche on the team. Although he was one of six Tiger hurlers with 15 or more starts, he led the staff with 47 games, good for fourth in the American League. His 32 relief appearances were also fourth in the league. More importantly, his six wins out of the bullpen led the league, and his seven saves were third best.

Tiger skipper Bucky Harris was among the first to recognize the usefulness of a bullpen stopper. Nearly a decade earlier, he had won back-to-back flags with Washington behind the pitching of the first great relief pitcher, Fred "Firpo" Marberry.

Harris and Marberry were reunited in Detroit in 1933, but Hogsett's presence enabled Fred to be used as a starter. Chief, meanwhile, was second in the league in relief appearances and also second in saves. He was ninth in saves in 1934 and second again in 1935. In all four years, he was the Detroit leader.

In both 1932 and 1935, he was the American League leader in relief wins and in 1933 he was second. In 1935, his 40 relief appearances topped the major leagues. For the four years—1932 through 1935—he was as good a reliever as there was in baseball.

But that ended in 1936. Hank Greenberg went down early and the Tigers needed a first baseman to defend the World Championship they had won in 1935. Jack Burns of the St. Louis Browns was available and the Brownies needed pitching, so on April 30 Chief was traded to St. Louis for Burns. Burns did a good job for Detroit, but, alas, he was no Greenberg. The loss of big Hank, coupled with the loss of their bullpen stopper and the loss of Mickey Cochrane later in the season, spelled doom for the Tigers' pennant defense.

Chief Hogsett, however, became the Browns' ace, winning 13 games for a very bad team. But he was well into his 30s by this time, and after the 1938 season he left the majors. He went on to enjoy several fine years in Triple-A ball. He even returned to Detroit for an encore at the age of 40 in 1944, as the war-depleted team was trying to form a pitching staff. He did well, too: three games, six and one-third innings, and a 0.00 ERA.

But that was it for Chief. He left baseball then after 20 years as a player, but he remains a fan and keeps up with the game.

*   *   *

BK: You joined the Tigers in 1929. What kind of minor league record did you have?

CHIEF HOGSETT: I'd had a pretty good year up in Montreal. I went there in 1929 and won 22 games and lost 12; I'm pretty sure that's the record. They [the Tigers] brought me up in September.

BK: How many years had you been in the minors?

CH: I started in professional baseball in 1925 with Cushing, Oklahoma, in that old Southwest League. It was a Class D league and those leagues were pretty short then.

That fall, when the league was over—Detroit had bought me during the '25 season—I was sent up to Toronto. Detroit worked with Toronto in those years. I finished 1925 with Toronto.

Detroit was working with Forth Worth at that time, too, in the Texas League, so they had me at Fort Worth in '26. I was only with 'em about a month, I guess, and they didn't like me so they sent me to east Texas—Marshall, Texas, in that East Texas League. I finished out the year with them.

In '27 I was with Decatur, Illinois, in the Three-I League. That was the year Lindbergh flew the ocean. Carl Hubbell was the other lefthander on the club then at Decatur. I'd won two or three ballgames, but they decided to keep Carl and they sent me to Wheeling, West Virginia, in the Mid-Atlantic League. I should have been a gypsy. (Laughs)

I finished the year with Wheeling and had a fair year and in '28 I wound up with Evansville, Indiana. I had a fair year down there. In fact, I was married in Evansville—my high school sweetheart.

I wound up with Montreal in 1929.

BK: The Tigers were one of the first teams to use a pitcher almost solely in relief and you were one of the first ones to be almost exclusively a relief pitcher.

CH: Yeah. Fred Marberry was the ace reliever at Washington. I think a couple of other teams had one. I was one of the first and we never got much credit in those days, either.

BK: Did you like relieving?

CH: Oh, I didn't mind it. I didn't know what the score was and didn't give a damn (laughs) as long as I was playing.

That fall [1929] when I came up I started a few times. I joined the Detroit club in Washington. I had my wife with me, coming from Montreal. Bucky Harris was the manager.

Earl Whitehill pitched the first game and I think he got beat, 2 to nothing. Then I think I pitched the second game. I got beat, 1 to nothing. Or vice-versa, it doesn't make a whole lot of difference. We didn't score a run all afternoon.

Then I was with Detroit all of '30 and then they got tired of me and figured I needed a little more minor league experience so they sent me to Toronto again. I think it was '31. I was there three or four weeks and they called me back and I was with them from then on.

BK: You had your best year as a Tiger in '32; you won 11 games and led the league with six wins in relief. And you batted .246 with two home runs. You were a good hitting pitcher.

CH: I was fast. I would dump one or drag one and carry the mail. I could go down that first base line pretty good.

BK: You hit six homers in your career. You weren't dumping those.

CH: I hit two one afternoon in Philadelphia off Tony Freitas. He was a little lefthanded pitcher that Connie Mack had. Tony got a couple in the middle of the plate. I know, because I used to get a couple in the middle of the plate every once in a while. (Laughs)

Sometimes I'd get them and sometimes they'd get me out, but in those days the team would usually have to get me in the beginning of the game—first inning or two. I'd get a little rough after that.

My old sinker ball would work pretty good at times. What they call the slider now was my curveball. I didn't know what a "slider" was.

BK: In '34 and '35 you were on two terrific teams. How good were they?

CH: Oh, we were *good*!

Hank Greenberg, you know, was the main hitter—and my old road roommate, Charlie Gehringer. We had a pretty good ballclub. We had Schoolboy Rowe and Tommy Bridges. And [Goose] Goslin. We made a deal with Washington—traded Johnny Stone, one of our outfielders.

BK: Do you think Tommy Bridges is Hall of Fame caliber?

CH: No. The reason, I think, is longevity—not long enough. Rowe may have been if he had lasted, but he had arm trouble.

BK: What do you think of your manager in those years?

CH: Mickey [Cochrane]? I pitched against him when he was with Philadelphia with Connie.

He'd catch me and I'd be pitching out there and experiment a little bit. I'd find it out pretty quick. I'd throw one ball and he'd step out in front of the plate and fire one back. "Cut that out!" I can just hear him. (Laughs)

He was a good manager, as long as he could play. Then after he got hit in the head and had to manage from the bench, he wasn't the same guy, they said. Of course, I was gone by that time. I'd been traded to the Browns.

BK: They had to trade you. Greenberg was hurt and they had no first baseman. They traded you for Jack Burns.

CH: We won the pennant in '34 and lost to the Cardinals [in the World Series] and we won in '35 and beat the Cubs [in the Series], and we'd have won in '36, too, but, as you say, Greenberg had his wrist broken and he couldn't play so they traded me.

Jack Burns was a good first baseman with the Browns but he didn't come through for Detroit. They [the Tigers] lost Hank and then they lost my services as a relief pitcher. They did finish second in '36, though.

BK: You pitched in both World Series in '34 and '35.

CH: I was in three games in the '34 World Series. I didn't get a decision.

Mickey told me in St. Louis, before we left to go back to Detroit to finish the Series, if it goes six games I was going to be the starter. It went seven games and I was in that seventh game and so were four other guys.

[Elden] Auker started and we all got clobbered. We were beaten before that game ever started. Walked in the clubhouse that day and you could hear a pin drop. We knew that ol' Diz [Dean] was going to pitch against us and knew that Hank couldn't hit either one of 'em with a ballpark full of bats. We got beat, 11 to nothing. There was five of us pitchers; we couldn't stop 'em.

The next year we beat the Cubs. Lonnie Warneke's arm went bad. I saw it drop. He was pitching a game against us and I was down in the bullpen watching. He hurt his arm on that pitch. They had a good ballclub.

I only pitched in one game. I was having a little trouble with my arm. Mickey put me in to relieve and he saw right away that I didn't have anything. I think he put in Schoolboy Rowe after me.

BK: When you joined the Browns in 1936, you became their number one starter.

CH: Rogers Hornsby was the manager then, and he let me start games and I think I won about 13 games.

I had a hell of a losing year, too. I lost, I think, 19. That was when Jim Bottomley was manager [in 1937].

BK: It was awfully easy to lose for the Browns.

CH: Yeah, it was, but they had some pretty good hitters.

No pitching. We'd walk one, then somebody'd boot one and we just didn't have strong enough pitching—none of us—to pitch out of our trouble.

BK: Harlond Clift, your third baseman in St. Louis—does he belong in the Hall of Fame?

CH: Harlond Clift was a good ballplayer. I don't know—there are

Chief Hogsett (George Brace photo).

probably some in there that don't deserve it any more than Harlond did. He was a good ballplayer, a good hustler, and all that.

Being on a team that gets noticed, I think that carries a lot of weight—a lot of consideration—on those decisions on Hall of Famers. But that's the way the ball bounces.

BK: You played at a time when perhaps the best hitters of all time played. Who was the best that you saw?

CH: Along about that time the Yankees' first five hitters were Earle Combs, the center fielder; he was lefthanded. Then they had Joey Sewell, their third baseman; he was lefthanded. And then came [Babe] Ruth and then came [Lou] Gehrig, then came Bill Dickey—they were all lefthanded. I kind of held my own with them.

But Dickey was rough, for a lefthander, because he could go down that line pretty good, you know. He'd dump one—drag one—and every once in a while he'd wrap up on one.

Gehrig was harder on me than Ruth was. I'd catch Ruth kind of sneaking back away from that plate two or three inches laying for my sinker. Oh, God, he hit one back at me one day at Yankee Stadium! If it had hit me, it would have decapitated me! I threw him a sinker. I shall never forget that play! He blistered it! And it hit second base just right to bounce up in Charlie Gehringer's hand. Of course, Charlie broke with the ball at the crack of the bat and Charlie threw him out before Babe was halfway to first base. He just stopped like he was shot and looks at me and put his hands on his hips and said, "You big SOB! I've got enough trouble with you without that!" (Laughs)

He'd always get his hits, but he never did get the long one off of me. He didn't murder me.

BK: Who was the toughest batter on you?

CH: Ossie Bluege, Washington third baseman. Hell, he could hit me blindfolded at midnight! He could hit me with a piece of baling wire. I threw him everything—change of pace, curve, my spinner, and everything else. (Laughs)

And Tony Lazzeri was tough on me.

BK: Considering everything—batting, fielding, and so on—who was the one best player of your time?

CH: I'll tell you the best all-around ballplayer I ever did see, all the years I played—and I broke him in—Joe DiMaggio. Boy, he could do everything!

He'd been hurt that spring—burned his leg with diathermy treatment—and I was with the Browns then. He came up. We knew he was a good hitter coming out of that [Pacific] Coast League.

I was fooling around there with him; I think he was hitting third or fourth. His first time at bat off me was a home run in old Sportsman's Park there in St. Louis. I was still in the game when he was up the second time. This time he hit to the retaining wall in center field—it hit right on top of that retaining wall. It bounced back in Sammy West's hands—held him to a triple that time.

That's when I started talking to myself. I figured I'd see whether he belonged there or not. I didn't throw at his head, but I gave him one around his belly to put him down. I thought if I could get him mad at me, I'd have a little better luck than home runs and triples, but he got up, just brushed himself off—didn't even look at me.

From then on, I threw him that little old tantalizing spinner that I had and kept him back off the plate once in a while. I had better luck with him then. He was the best all-around player I ever saw.

I was pitching the game that Bob Feller broke in—1936. We had Cleveland beat, 8 to 2 or something like that. The manager put Bob in there to finish up the last two innings. He was scared to death, naturally, like we all were when we broke in. He was just as apt to throw back of a hitter as he was in front of him. He stayed in the game until the finish.

We left and went on the road. About two or three weeks after that Bob started against us. I think he struck out 16 or 17 of us then. That hitter had to be alert! He hit a guy or two in the head, if I remember accurately.

He was *wild*! Geez, he was wild! But he had a lot of stuff.

BK: Was he the best pitcher you saw?

CH: He had a terrific curveball and he had a terrific fastball.

Walter Johnson was managing the Cleveland ballclub when I came up. He'd pitch batting practice and he could throw that thing pretty good then.

They said he was a kind of tough manager to work for, about like Hornsby. Hornsby thought all those hitters ought to be as good as he was. Walter Johnson was the same.

BK: Is there a game you remember especially—your best game or biggest thrill?

CH: Brent, I can't think right now what I could pick out. I think the first game when I got beat at Washington. I don't know. The Series games were a thrill. It was just nice to be there.

BK: It's been nearly 70 years since you became a professional ballplayer.

CH: It's a little different school, financial-wise.

BK: What was your best salary?

CH: Seventy-five hundred. You could buy a middle-sized Buick car and go to Florida every winter on that, too. I don't think you can get to Georgia on that today.

It's ridiculous—the money. But what the hell isn't ridiculous today?

And meal money is up around $65 a day. I take *The Sporting News* and kind of keep up with it. I read it all the time. It doesn't do me a hell of a lot of good to read anymore. (Laughs) I catch myself reading a whole paragraph and be thinking of something else and I'll say, "What the hell was in that paragraph?" and I'll have to go back and read it over.

They made me and the old 1903 Springfield rifle the same year.

BK: That makes you one of the oldest living ex-ballplayers.

CH: I don't know about that, but there's only about five of us left that were in that '35 World Series. But the game stays in the blood.

BK: Are you still fairly active?

CH: I lost my wife about 15 years ago, so I'm all alone now. I've got my own ways and do my own work—mow my yard.

I have two children. My daughter's my first child; she was born in Detroit. She teaches school down in Great Bend [Kansas], and she comes home once in a while and helps me out a little.

The second child is Stanley. He's a doctor with the Veterans Administration back in Danville, Illinois. He was born in Minneapolis.

The "Itis" family moved in on me a year or two ago. Old Arther's got my left shoulder and Burs' got my right knee.

BK: You were with Washington in 1938, then you went to Triple-A for about five years.

CH: I went back to Minneapolis for Mike Kelly. That was the American Association then. I went there from the Old Fox's [Clark Griffith] nest in Washington and I had a pretty good year.

I had a contract there that if I was traded or sold back to the big leagues I'd get a little bonus—$1,500, I think it was. That's the pennies we dealt with in those days.

Well, Connie Mack drafted me [in 1940], I think on account of the two home runs I hit against his lefthanded pitcher. I don't think he drafted me on account of my pitching. Of course, I pitched pretty good against the Athletics in those days.

I trained with him out in Anaheim, California, that spring. I wanted more money from him and he wouldn't give it to me. "Come on out; we'll fix it up when you get out here." Of course, I knew what the score would be there, too. (Laughs) On the way East after spring training, he turned me back to Minneapolis.

The Tigers brought me up again in '44, during the war. That was when they had [Hal] Newhouser and Dizzy Trout. They had some pretty good pitching then. Steve O'Neill was the manger at that time.

I was in pretty good shape when spring training ended. We had our spring training in Evansville, Indiana, that year. But we had the good pitching and I didn't get any work for three or four weeks. They let me go and sent me back to Minneapolis. Forty-four was the last year I even tried to pitch.

BK: What did you do when you left baseball?

CH: I had a job selling liquor up in Minneapolis and I went with a fly-by-night sporting good outfit. All you had to have during the war was a $1,000 and you could become a jobber—a wholesaler. I went out and sold stuff and back order, back order, back order. So I didn't do much good aside from spending my own money there.

Then I quit there and moved back to Kansas. I was broke and I couldn't find a job for quite a little while when I got back to Kansas. Then I finally got a job selling liquor, covering the whole northwest part of the state.

I've been retired now for about 25 years now.

BK: Did you save souvenirs from your career?

CH: Very, very, very few. I get a lot of requests for memorabilia, but, no, I saved very little.

I do have something—I've got a baseball autographed by the Babe. I can't remember what year it was; in those years on our autographs we didn't date anything. It was either '30 or '31. The baseballs then had red, white, and blue threading on them. It's authentic, I know that, because I got it myself, but it's not dated.

I date all mine and right today I get a lot of requests from all over the country. I sign all of 'em, don't charge 'em for it either. Some of those idiots charge for their autographs. That's ridiculous.

Once in a great while, I get a dollar bill in a request for an autograph. I send it back.

I had some pictures my wife had made, but I don't have any anymore. But I sign anything anybody sends.

BK: If you went back, would you play baseball again?

CH: That's a hypothetical question. I suppose I would. I was born on a farm, grew up on a farm, and I *hated* the farm.

I could throw. When I was a kid, I don't think I ever passed a rock that I didn't pick up and throw.

Twenty years I was in the racket; I enjoyed it all. Sometimes I'd get the hell knocked out of me—knocked out of the box and stuff—that goes with the territory.

Elon Chester (Chief) Hogsett

Born November 2, 1903, Brownell, KS
Ht. 6′ Wt. 190 Batted and Threw Left

Year	Team	G	IP	W	L	PCT	BB	SO	H	SHO	SV	ERA
1929	DetA	4	28.2	1	2	.333	9	9	34	1	0	2.83
1930		33	146	9	8	.529	63	54	174	0	1	5.42
1931		22	112.1	3	9	.250	33	47	150	0	2	5.93
1932		47	178	11	9	.550	66	56	201	0	7	3.54
1933		45	116	6	10	.375	56	39	137	0	9	4.50

In the Shadow of the Babe

Year	Team	G	IP	W	L	PCT	BB	SO	H	SHO	SV	ERA
1934		26	50.1	3	2	.600	19	23	61	0	3	4.29
1935		40	96.2	6	6	.500	49	39	109	0	5	3.54
1936	DetA	3	4	0	1	.000	1	1	8	0	0	9.00
	StLA	39	215.1	13	15	.464	90	67	278	0	1	5.52
1937	StLA	37	177.1	6	19	.240	75	68	245	1	2	6.29
1938	WasA	31	91	5	6	.455	36	33	107	0	3	6.03
1944	DetA	3	6.1	0	0	.000	4	5	7	0	0	0.00
11 years		330	1222	63	87	.420	501	441	1511	2	33	5.02

World Series

Year	Team	G	IP	W	L	PCT	BB	SO	H	SHO	SV	ERA
1934	DetA	3	7.1	0	0	.000	3	3	6	0	0	1.23
1935		1	1	0	0	.000	1	0	0	0	0	0.00
2 years		4	8.1	0	0	.000	4	3	6	0	0	1.08

GUS SUHR

National League Iron Horse

1930–1940

On the evening of September 11, 1931, after the day's games were over, the major league record for consecutive games played was held by Everett Scott with 1,307. But Lou Gehrig, with 870, was narrowing the gap daily.

Scott and Gehrig were American Leaguers. Over in the National League, Eddie Brown held the record with 618, but Gus Suhr was gaining

***Above:* Gus Suhr (George Brace photo).**

on him. At the close of play on September 11, 1931, Suhr had played one game in a row.

Nothing or no one could get Suhr out of the lineup from then on. From then through June 4, 1937—five-and-a-half years—he matched Gehrig game for game and may have gone on longer, but he took himself out of the lineup when his mother died. The streak ended at 822 games, a new National League record and fourth best ever at that time. Today, over a half century later, Suhr's 822 is still ninth best (fourth in the National League). Only once during the streak—on June 20, 1935—was his streak "helped"; he played one inning in the outfield after hurting his hand the day before.

Gus Suhr's streak began at the end of his second season with the Pirates, a season which was otherwise extremely forgettable. After a brilliant rookie year in 1930 (17 HR, 107 RBIs, 14 triples, 93 runs, 80 walks), he was injured early in 1931 and never got back on track that year. That season was the only blemish on a stellar decade as Pittsburgh's first baseman.

Suhr was well prepared for his record-breaking streak. In 1929 with the San Francisco Seals in the PCL, he played every inning in his club's 202 games. And he had one of the finest seasons ever in a league noted for fine seasons: he hit 51 home runs, drove in 177, batted .381 (with 299 hits), and scored 196 runs. (Surprisingly, only his runs scored led the league.) In the three years, from 1927 through 1929, Gus played in 588 of 589 games. Durability was his long suit.

The 1929 season was his fourth full year with the hometown Seals. A natural first baseman, when he joined them in 1926 that position was occupied by Bert "Babe" Ellison, an ex-major leaguer and long-time Seal, who was also the team's manager. Gus was a righthanded thrower and too good a hitter not to play, so he was moved to second base.

Ellison was gone the next season, but the Seals had acquired Hollis Thurston, erstwhile pitcher and outstanding hitter. Their bats dictated that both Suhr and Thurston be in the lineup. Because Gus was the better fielder, he remained at second base.

But in 1929, first base was finally his, just as it was in Pittsburgh throughout the 1930s.

There are a few other highlights to Gus Suhr's career, beside his durability and consistency:

- On April 29, 1930, he walked five times in a game. That tied the modern (since 1900) major league record and has not been broken.
- His 107 RBIs in 1930 were, at the time, the third most by a modern National League rookie. It is still sixth.
- In 1934, his seven unassisted double plays set a major league record for first basemen. Jim Bottomley also had seven that year.

- He had a 1.66:1 walk to strikeout ratio for his career (718 BB, 433 K).
- He set a NL record with 70 consecutive errorless games.
- He led the NL first basemen in double plays three times.

* * *

BK: You signed with the San Francisco Seals in 1925 and were there for only a cup of coffee.

GUS SUHR: Yeah. I was 19 years old when I first signed. I worked out there with the Seals, and then they sent me to Quincy, Illinois [III League], as a first baseman.

BK: Why did they switch you to second base?

GS: It was actually shortstop. They had a second baseman; they had [Pete] Kilduff and they had Bert Ellison on first base and then they had [Ed] Mulligan at third base, and that left the shortstop because Hal Rhyne went up that year. It was a battle for shortstop really. There were three of us there. One was Knobby Paynter and the second was Roddy Zafael and then there was me. (Laughs) I was the third one and I was shipped out to Quincy, where I played first base.

BK: When you returned to San Francisco after the year at Quincy, you were a middle infielder again.

GS: It took me a long time to get back to first base, Herb Ellison was the manager. (Laughs) He was a good ballplayer, though.

BK: Your play improved each year with San Francisco until, finally, in 1929, you couldn't get any better. [Yearly RBI and BA: 1926—71, .282; 1927—118, .293; 1928—133, .314; 1929—177, .381.]

GS: The '29 season I played in every game, every inning of every game, 201 or 2 games. And the year before that I played in 191. And 195 before that. (Laughs)

BK: Ike Boone with Portland won the Triple Crown in '29.

GS: Yeah, I guess he did. He was up there, anyway. I was maybe third or fourth [in batting] because we had a big fella by the name of [Smead] Jolley. He beat me out by a couple of points, I think.

BK: How did the Pirates acquire you?

GS: The scout for 'em—his name was Joe Devine—he followed me and he signed me up. The last year I played first base with the Seals and they made the deal after the season. I don't know how much they paid for me.

BK: In looking at your fielding stats, it appears that you were an adequate second baseman but a doggone good first baseman. Is that safe to say?

GS: Yeah, that would be safe.

BK: 1930 was your rookie season in Pittsburgh and you had an outstanding year. Did you have an adjustment problem at all?

GS: No, I didn't. I just kept playing, you know, when they wanted me to. They just left me alone.

BK: What about Forbes Field for a lefthanded batter? If you hit it right down the line, it wasn't much, but if you got it five feet off the line it was a country mile out there. Did that affect you?

GS: I guess it did to some extent. I'd hit the ball well a lot of times and it would be caught. You know, the place where I played in San Francisco [Recreation Park] was a short right field fence. That was about 270 feet or so to the right fence so I got a lot of home runs there.

BK: Pop flies went over, but a well hit ball ended up as a double.

GS: Yeah, that's right. And you had to run like a son of a gun to get it, too. (Laughs)

BK: You *could* run [league-leading 64 doubles in 1928, 62 more in 1929]. You hit a lot of doubles and triples.

GS: Yeah, I could run a little bit. The fences in Forbes Field helped me there.

BK: You had such a good rookie year; what happened in '31?

GS: I got hurt right off the bat—about three weeks into the season. I was out for a *long* time and then I finally made it in. I didn't do so hot, did I? (Laughs)

BK: No, but once you got back in the lineup they couldn't get you out of it for years. You were remarkably durable and set the NL record for consecutive games played.

GS: I went out because my mother passed away. That's why the streak was broken, otherwise I would've been playin' a few more games, I know that.

BK: You had an excellent walk-to-strikeout ratio. Did you always have a good eye or was it something you developed?

GS: I had a pretty good eye at first. I thought I did pretty well at getting on first base by drawing a walk.

BK: A ratio like yours is almost unheard of today. They walk 30 times and strikeout 120.

GS: (Laughs) Geez, look at the money they get, too.

BK: What was your top salary?

GS: It was a little bit better than ten, I think.

BK: You had an infield there in Pittsburgh for a couple of years: you, Pep Young, Arky Vaughan, Pie Traynor. Was that the best infield in the league then?

Gus Suhr (courtesy National Pastime).

GS: At that time, Pie, I think he had a bad arm then. He wasn't quite the fielder he was when he had his good arm. He'd get rid of the ball so damn fast you'd be runnin' to first base with your eye on the ball. (Laughs) He was good. Oh yeah. He made the fantastic plays and get rid of the ball so *fast*—that was one of his major things. He could get rid of that ball soon as it was hit to him. You had to be on your toes at first base to catch it.

BK: Arky Vaughan was a long time getting into the Hall of Fame, but it was very much deserved.

GS: Oh yes! So much so. He was good. He could hit, too. He was sure a good one.

BK: The Waner brothers.

GS: Oh, they were great! Paul and Lloyd—they were both great, especially Paul, you know. He got on base many a time. He could hit 'em with anybody.

BK: In 1935, Babe Ruth had his last big game against you guys.

GS: His next to last game he played was against us. We were playin' at Pittsburgh. He didn't play the whole game, either. He got three home runs and played to the eighth inning, I think. Two of 'em were hit *really* hard. He hit three home runs and darned if we didn't beat 'em, 11 to 8. (Laughs) [Ruth's last home run—his third of the day and 714th of his career—cleared the right field grandstand at Forbes Field. It was the first ever to do so and was measured at 600 feet.] The old boy, he must've been something to see 'cause I saw him when he was through and he still hit three home runs. (Laughs)

BK: Who was the best player you saw?

GS: Oh, I don't know. Maybe Paul Waner was. There were some good ones, though. St. Louis had that [Joe] Medwick and they had Bottomley. Cincinnati, they had [Frank] McCormick—he could hit. New York, they had Frankie Frisch and [Mel] Ott and that first baseman—he was a great hitter—[Bill] Terry. He was a dandy. Seems each team had more good players than the whole league does now.

BK: Who was the best pitcher you saw?

GS: The best pitcher, in my opinion, was that lefthander for St. Louis. That was [Bill] Hallahan. Dizzy Dean was up there. Carl Hubbell. They were *real* good, too. And then the Brooklyn Dodgers had a lefthander by the name of Watty Clark. Hallahan was just about the toughest on me. He pitched good ball for a long time.

BK: You were selected for the All-Star team in '36 and didn't play. You had much better stats than Ripper Collins, who played the whole game.

GS: I don't know about that. Charlie Grimm was managing our [NL] team and he had a lot of starters for the Cubs there. They didn't win for three games, so he thought he'd better play them. (Laughs) I think he only changed pitchers once or twice.

BK: You were remarkably consistent for years. Why weren't you chosen for other All-Star games?

GS: I don't know. They had some good first basemen. They had Dolph

Camilli there and they had the first baseman for Cincinnati [McCormick]—he was real good. And Bottomley and Mize.

BK: Is there a game that stands out in your memory?

GS: It happened in '38 and we played a doubleheader in Pittsburgh against the Giants and they beat us the first game. In the second game we had Sunday labor laws or somethin' and it was gettin' kinda late in that second game and we were gettin' beat by a run. Came the ninth inning and our last time up—I knew we couldn't play much longer—and the tying run was on second base and two outs and I was up. This righthanded pitcher—I don't remember his name now, it happened so long ago, you know—he threw two strikes by me and then he threw a ball. Then he threw another one up there and I hit this one to right field and the tying run came in.

BK: The Pirates traded you to the Phillies in 1939 for Max Butcher. Why?

GS: Geez, I don't know. Seemed like they wanted to get rid of a player and they got rid of me. I felt kinda bad, but that's the way she goes.

BK: That was pretty much the end of the line.

GS: They [Phillies] let me go [in 1940]. I went up to Montreal and finished the season up there. I played in '43, '44, and '45 for the Seals. In '48 I managed in the minors and that was it.

BK: Did you save souvenirs from your career?

GS: No, I never did. I haven't a glove or pair of spikes or anything left.

BK: Do you still get fan mail?

GS: Not too much, but I seem to get it more now than ever. I sign.

BK: Any regrets from your career?

GS: Oh no, not much. I just went along with what they told me.

BK: Would you play baseball again?

GS: Oh, I think I would. I'd play it. Maybe I'd get a little bit more money. (Laughs) They get by these dollar signs so fast now.

August Richard Suhr

Born January 3, 1906, San Francisco, CA
Ht. 6′ Wt. 180 Batted Left and Threw Right

Year	Team	G	AB	R	H	2B	3B	HR	RBI	SB	BA	SA
1930	PitN	151	542	93	155	26	14	17	107	11	.286	.480
1931		87	270	26	57	13	4	4	32	4	.211	.333
1932		154	581	78	153	31	16	5	81	7	.263	.398
1933		154	566	72	151	31	11	10	75	2	.267	.413
1934		151	573	67	162	36	13	13	103	4	.283	.459

Year	Team	G	AB	R	H	2B	3B	HR	RBI	SB	BA	SA
1935		153	529	68	144	33	12	10	81	6	.272	.437
1936		156	583	111	182	33	12	11	118	8	.312	.467
1937		151	575	69	160	28	14	5	97	2	.278	.402
1938		145	530	82	156	35	14	3	64	4	.294	.430
1939	PitN	63	204	23	59	10	2	1	31	4	.289	.373
	PhiN	60	198	21	63	12	2	3	24	1	.318	.444
1940	PhiN	10	25	4	4	0	0	2	5	0	.160	.400
11 years		1435	5176	714	1446	288	114	84	818	53	.279	.428

GENE DESAUTELS

Holy Cross Crusader

1930–1946

The Eastern College Athletic Conference (ECAC) is primarily thought of for its basketball today. Long winters limit the length of baseball schedules and the ability of the schools in the conference to attract top

Above: **Gene Desautels (George Brace photo).**

prospects; most players prefer to go south or west to pursue the game and continue their educations.

Holy Cross College (officially, College of the Holy Cross) is a small, Roman Catholic–affiliated, coeducational member of the ECAC located in Worcester, Massachusetts. Enrollment is only about 2,500. In spite of its size and location, Holy Cross has been among the major collegiate sources of outstanding baseball talent; dozens of Crusaders have reached the major leagues.

Among the first was Jack Barry, the shortstop in Connie Mack's "$100,000 Infield" of the early teens. In 1921, Barry returned to his alma mater as the head baseball coach. Over the next 40 years he produced such ballplayers as Pat Bourque, Lennie Merullo, Dave Stenhouse, Al Niemiec, Mike Hegan, Bots Nekola, and Gene Desautels.

In fact, Nekola, a southpaw, and Desautels formed Holy Cross's battery in the late 1920s, until Bots gave up his final year of eligibility to sign with the Yankees. His major league career was short and undistinguished, but his contribution turned out to be outstanding nonetheless. He was a Red Sox scout for 27 years and among his signees were Carl Yastrzemski, Rico Petrocelli, and Ben Oglivie.

Desautels, however, went on to enjoy a 13-year major league career as a catcher. An unremarkable hitter, he nevertheless spent four years as the number one backstop for the Red Sox and, afterward, he kept his spot on a major league roster with his defensive skills and ability to handle young pitchers.

Desautels turned to managing in the minors when his playing days were over. He was fairly successful for several years until fate placed him in command of the horrible Sacramento Solons of the Pacific Coast League in 1953 and 1954. It was a franchise nearly bankrupt, both in money and talent, and it became Gene's last active stop in baseball.

His love for baseball remained and he enjoyed talking about it.

* * *

BK: What team originally signed you?

GENE DESAUTELS: Originally I signed with Detroit. They signed me out of college.

BK: College educated ballplayers were pretty uncommon then.

GD: I don't know. There were quite a few.

Bots Nekola signed with the Yankees before I signed. He was in my class. He left school a year ahead of time.

BK: You began with Detroit but then spent some time in the minors.

GD: When Mickey Cochrane came I had been with Detroit for three years. Then I went to Toledo, that was one year, and then I went out to the coast for two years, so I was in the minors—Triple-A—for three years.

BK: What kind of minor league record did you have?

GD: At Toledo I did not have a good record. My first year on the coast, with Hollywood, I did not have a good year, but then the next year at San Diego, I had a good year and that's when Boston bought me.

BK: You came to Boston in 1937 and in '38 you had an excellent season.

GD: I just happened to get hot. I was never a good hitter, but I had a good year that year. I hit .291 and I caught in over 100 games. I just learned to hit a curve ball when I was out in the Coast League, when I was with San Diego, especially.

I should have gone out [to the minors] earlier, but they [the Tigers] never sent me out.

BK: Over your career, you were hard to strike out [once every 12 at bats], so you must have been getting a piece of the curve all along.

GD: I always got a piece of the ball—I was a contact hitter. I didn't have the power to go for long balls.

BK: You were pretty much the number one catcher all four years with the Red Sox.

GD: Yeah. When I went there, Rick Ferrell was there, but then they got rid of him and I got to be first string catcher for three years, at least. Then I went to Cleveland.

BK: Who was in that trade?

GD: When I went to Cleveland from Boston, Jim Bagby and Gee Walker came with me. Boston got [Frankie] Pytlak and somebody else [Odell Hale and Joe Dobson] from Cleveland.

BK: You got to catch some pretty good pitchers in Cleveland—Bob Feller and Mel Harder.

GD: Oh, yeah. They were two good ones.

BK: You were with the Indians for three years and then went into the service in 1944.

GD: I went to the service for a year and a half. I came back in the fall of '45.

BK: Did you play ball in the service?

GD: I played some, but I managed the Paris Island baseball team for two summers. I was in the Marine Corps.

BK: Was that your first managing experience?

GD: Yeah, that was the first.

BK: When you returned, you played for the Philadelphia Athletics in 1946 and then you left the major leagues.

GD: I went to Toronto and played a year there. That was the International League. Then I went to managing.

BK: Where?

GD: I managed first at Williamsport, Pennsylvania, for two years, then I came to Flint [Michigan] for one year, and then I went to Little Rock for a year and we won the pennant there. Then I managed for Hank Greenberg at Indianapolis for one year. I knew that he had Birdie Tebbetts coming there. I was just an interim manager.

Then he [Greenberg] got me the job of Sacramento. When I went there, I realized they had nothing. They were operating on a shoestring. They couldn't afford to buy anybody or get anybody. And that was it for managing.

BK: Who was the best player you saw?

GD: All around player? Joe DiMaggio.

BK: Who was the best hitter?

GD: Oh, Ted Williams was the best hitter. But DiMaggio could run, he could hit, he could throw. He was the best all-around player that I played against.

BK: Who was the best pitcher you saw?

GD: They were all good, as far as I was concerned. (Laughs)

When I came up to Boston I started catching Lefty Grove. He was still a great pitcher but he had lost his fastball. He had a lot of savvy as a pitcher—he knew what he was doing. He was still a great pitcher until he quit.

Of course, I caught Bob Feller for a year and a half, two years in Cleveland.

And I caught a lot of other great pitchers like, when I was with Detroit, I caught Earl Whitehill. When I first came out of college—I think it was the second week—I caught Whitehill. He was a lefthanded pitcher and he won 11 straight games in that season [1930]. Up until that time he had only won two games [that season] so they gave me some credit for catching him. I was able to handle lefthanded pitchers.

BK: You played under several different managers. Who do you consider the best?

GD: I played under Bucky Harris at Detroit and then at Boston I played under Joe Cronin and at Cleveland I played under [Lou] Boudreau and [Roger] Peckinpaugh and then, of course, I was with Connie Mack in my last year in '47 at Philadelphia. I wouldn't want to pick one of them; they were all good managers, I thought.

Bucky Harris was a good manager, but he lacked some experience.

Gene Desautels (courtesy National Pastime).

BK: Rather than the best, which manager do you feel had the most influence on you?

GD: I've got to give them all credit. I think Bucky Harris did a lot for me because he liked me as a catcher and maybe he, as a major league manager, did more for me than anyone.

The fellow that helped me more than anything was before I went to the big leagues—my coach at Holy Cross College, Jack Barry. He taught me a lot of baseball.

BK: Is there one game that stands out in your memory?

GD: I've got a couple of games. I caught Lefty Grove Opening Day, 1938, I think. I caught his one-hitter and that hit they got was doubtful. That stood out.

And when I was with Detroit, Tom Bridges graduated from the University of Tennessee the same month and he joined the Tigers the same day as I did. About two weeks later, we were the battery against the Yankees in Yankee Stadium. That was quite a thrill, going up against Babe Ruth and Gehrig and Lazzeri and Crosetti and so many great ballplayers.

We were ahead, 3 to 2, going into the ninth inning. When they came to bat, we got two out and Gehrig walked and then who comes up but the Babe. We got two strikes on him and Bucky Harris, who was the manager, called time and called us out to the mound and said, "Now, look. Be careful, because this guy is dangerous at all times." He told us what to do. He told Tommy. "Next pitch that you throw I want you to brush him back right under his chin so he can't touch the ball and then come back with a curve and see if you can strike him out."

We went back and I called for a fastball inside and Tom didn't get it high enough and Babe hit it for a home run and they beat us, 4 to 3. That was tough.

BK: You hit three home runs in your career. Do you remember any of them?

GD: I hit one against Red Ruffing—I won't forget that! It was in New York when I played for Cleveland. In fact, I won the ballgame for Cleveland that day.

I hit one in Washington, I hit one in Boston. I was *not* a home run hitter. (Laughs)

BK: It's been 60 years since you became a professional ballplayer. What's the biggest change in the game?

GD: The biggest change? (Laughs) The biggest change is what happened with television. That's why the players are getting so much money now.

Another change is the big change in gloves. All the Tiger alumni were up at Drummond Island—that's [Tom] Monaghan's [ex–Tiger owner] place—and we were playing a softball game. The gloves are just like big nets. When I played, for example, Lou Boudreau had a glove that would just fit his hand. But he had a great pair of hands. These outfielders today play with gloves that are almost nets!

The fields are so much better, too. When I played in Detroit in 1930 the fields were not like they are now. I remember Bill Rogell and a lot of us used to go around the infield picking up pebbles before the game.

BK: Did you save souvenirs from your career?

GD: I did have a lot of souvenirs, but I gave 'em all away. I had about 15 baseballs signed by Babe Ruth, and I gave them all away to kids. I found out later that the kids used 'em to play ball with.

BK: Did you keep anything?

GD: Not many things. My wife's got pictures and stuff like that.

BK: Do you receive much fan mail?

GD: I get letters every week for autographs or pictures or something like that.

BK: Do you sign autographs?

GD: Oh, yeah.

BK: What do you think of players charging for their autographs?

GD: I think it's awful! I think players that are charging five, ten, fifteen dollars are terrible. Every time I see [Pete] Rose sitting down and autographing baseballs for ten or fifteen dollars I think it's terrible. And look what's happened to him. They get so greedy.

BK: If you went back to your Holy Cross days, would you be a professional ballplayer again?

GD: I loved baseball. Babe Ruth was one of my idols. That's why I got such a thrill catching against him about two weeks after I got out of college.

I think I would. I loved baseball so much. I always wanted to be a ballplayer.

Eugene Abraham (Red) Desautels

Born June 7, 1907, Worcester, MA
Died November 5, 1994, Flint, MI
Ht. 5'11" Wt. 170 Batted and Threw Right

Year	Team	G	AB	R	H	2B	3B	HR	RBI	SB	BA	SA
1930	DetA	42	126	13	24	4	2	0	9	2	.190	.254
1931		3	11	1	1	0	0	0	0	0	.091	.091
1932		28	72	8	17	2	0	0	2	0	.236	.264
1933		30	42	5	6	1	0	0	4	0	.143	.167
1937	BosA	96	305	33	74	10	3	0	27	1	.243	.295
1938		108	333	47	97	16	2	2	48	1	.291	.369
1939		76	226	26	55	14	0	0	21	3	.243	.305
1940		71	222	19	50	7	1	0	17	0	.225	.266
1941	CleA	66	189	20	38	5	1	1	17	1	.201	.254
1942		62	162	14	40	5	0	0	9	1	.247	.278
1943		68	185	14	38	6	1	0	19	2	.205	.249
1945		10	9	1	1	0	0	0	0	0	.111	.111
1946	PhiA	52	130	10	28	3	1	0	13	1	.215	.254
13 years		712	1012	211	469	73	11	3	186	12	.233	.285

BILL WERBER

"Tiger"

1930–1942

The 1937 Cincinnati Reds were a bad team. They really had not been a good team for more than a decade. The 1937 team finished in the cellar, 5½ games out of seventh; it was the fifth last-place finish in seven years for the club. The last time the Reds had finished in the first division was in 1926 and things were not looking good for baseball in the Queen City as the 1930s entered their final stages.

Above: **Bill Werber (George Brace photo).**

A new manager was named for 1938, however. Bill McKechnie took over for Bobby Wallace, who had replaced Chuck Dressen the previous September. McKechnie wasted no time; he overhauled the team, and the Reds had many new faces in the everyday lineup in 1938.

It was a better team entering the season, but it was still short of first-division quality. McKechnie continued to make changes. A week into the season, Jim Weaver was purchased from the Browns. Then in June, two major trades were made. On June 6, young second baseman Alex Kampouris was sent to the Giants for veteran outfielder Wally Berger. On the thirteenth, Spud Davis, Al Hollingsworth, and $50,000 went to the Phillies for Bucky Walters. The end result was a fourth-place finish, 28 games better than 1937 and only six games behind the National League champion Cubs.

McKechnie made a couple of more changes for 1939. One was the addition of rookie righthander Junior Thompson (now known as Gene), who joined the pitching staff and went 13-5, with a 2.55 ERA. The other, and the reason (regardless of what he says) the Reds won the pennant, was the acquisition of veteran third baseman Bill Werber from the A's. Werber became available when Connie Mack would not give him a $1,500 raise.

Werber had been a solid performer in the American League for six years; his chief contributions had been stolen bases (he led the league three times) and hustle. In 1939 with the Reds he did not suddenly develop a home run stroke or a penchant for RBIs. In fact, his stats in those two categories were his lowest since his rookie year. Statistically there wasn't much difference in his production and that of 1938's third baseman, Lew Riggs. He did, however, lead the National League in runs (115) and had the second-highest number of stolen bases (15). But these were not his biggest contributions, either.

Where Bill Werber contributed, and therefore made the difference between a fourth-place team and one that won the pennant, was on defense. Had there been a Gold Glove award in 1939, he probably would have won it. He led National League basemen in assists, double plays, total chances per game (range), and errors, and was second in putouts. That alone, however, is not going to account for a team improving 12 games in the standings, even if the previous year's third sacker had not worn a glove.

Werber's biggest contribution was in changing the attitude of the rest of the Reds' infield. In the interview which follows, Bill tells of the "Jungle Club," where he challenged, encouraged, and maybe even intimidated his fellow infielders into playing on a different level. And he led by example. The results: a team which had been near the bottom in fielding in 1938 was now second in the league, a team which had been *last* in double plays was now second, and an infield which had been sixth in total chances was now first.

Any pitcher will tell you that his success (and his ERA) is as much a function of his team as it is of his own ability. The Reds' infield in 1939 averaged four more chances a game than the Reds' infield in 1938. How to interpret these four chances is open to debate, but what can be seen in black and white is the fact that the staff's ERA went from 3.62 (fifth in the league) to 3.27 (first in the National League).

Yet Bill Werber claims he was not National League's Most Valuable Player in 1939 (teammate Walters was and four other Reds received more votes than Werber, making him sixth on his own team). But where would the Reds have been without him? Not in the World Series.

* * *

BK: You were Duke University's first All-American basketball player. Was there any temptation to play pro basketball?

BILL WERBER: No, there was no temptation to play pro basketball. In 1930, when I graduated from Duke, pro basketball did not have the same stature that pro baseball had, nor did it pay the same money. And it didn't have the same organization, so I was not inclined to go into basketball at all.

BK: Wasn't pro basketball at that time very loose-knit and sort of restricted to industrial leagues and YMCAs and that type of thing?

BW: Yes, it was. As a matter of fact, George Marshall, who owned the Palace Laundry in Washington, D.C., had most of the original Celtics there in Washington playing for him. He had Dutch Dehnert and Pete Barry and Horse Haggerty and Nat Holman. He had those people there, and I was playing basketball at Tech High School at the time and we used to go the Arcade and scrimmage against those players. George Marshall, who later owned the Redskins, had a team but they were more or less a freelance organization that scheduled contests here, there, and elsewhere, and it really wasn't as complete a league as it later developed into.

BK: In high school, you scrimmaged against that quality of player?

BW: Oh yes. They had a big net that fastened down into the floor and those players used to toss us into the net like beanbags. (Laughs) They taught us a great deal about how basketball should be played. They taught us just about every dirty trick in the book—holding onto your pants and holding onto your belt, locking their elbows over your arm and, if there was a trick in basketball, when I went to Duke Univeristy I knew it because I'd played against many of the original Celtics. Course, they were much larger, much heavier, and they were much more experienced than we were, but it was good training for us.

BK: After graduation, you began law school. Did you finish?

BW: No, I did not. When I got through with Duke and my first year of baseball, I entered Georgetown law school and I had a year of law school and did very well. During the latter part of my law school year, the Yankees came to me and asked me whether I intended to continue with law school or whether I was going to play ball. I had no money, I had a wife—I'd been married back in September of 1929—I had a little boy that was born on January 8th, 1931, and I had to have the money to feed these people, so I told the Yankees I was going to play ball. I was reasonably successful in baseball and it took me a long time before I was able to work myself out of it, but I always worked toward getting *out* of baseball. I really never did work to stay in it. And, ultimately, I was able to get out of baseball but it did take me about 12 years to do it.

I was reasonably successful and did command one of the higher salaries and in those days—there was a big depression in 1929, '30, and '31—I was making as much or more than college presidents, and it was hard to turn your back on that kind of money.

BK: How much?

BW: 12,500 to 13,000. It was a lot of money.

BK: You were a team leader every where you played. Did you ever consider managing?

BW: No. I was working all the time to get out of baseball. I wasn't interested in staying in it. I enjoyed it, I had a good time, I liked the players, it was a lot of fun, but I was more family-oriented and I didn't like to travel, I didn't like moving the children from school to school and I wanted to establish roots for the kids in school, and I just didn't like moving around. And I was interested in getting into business. Baseball was a game to me. (Laughs) I enjoyed it, I had fun with it, and I was happy to move on to something else. I didn't make a big fuss about leaving—call a press conference or anything—I just cleaned out my locker and went home.

BK: Paul Krichell signed you. For how much?

BW: It was a rather peculiar arrangement. Actually, I never signed anything with the Yankees. I talked with Paul Krichell. I had no money. The Yankees agreed to finance my sophomore, junior, and senior years, they agreed to pay me a bonus at the time I actually *did* sign a contract. The man laid it out orally for me, I told him that the offer sounded good to me. I told him that I would go along on that basis and that after graduation I *would* sign a contract and I *would* agree to play with the Yankees and that the terms and conditions were satisfactory to me. I looked him in the eye, he looked me in the eye, we shook hands and that was all there was ever to it. There was nothing ever signed; I believed the man and the man believed me.

About three or four days after all of this happened, my father was approached by Arthur Devlin, with whom he had played in the Washington area, and Arthur Devlin was scouting for the Giants and he offered twice as much money as the Yankees had offered. I told my dad that I had agreed to go with the Yankees and how much money they had offered. My dad said if you agreed to do that, then that ends it. That's the way that my dad was accustomed to doing business and that's the way I've always been accustomed to doing business. If I tell you that I'm going to do something, that ends it.

BK: That's the way it should be done, yet today these guys want to renegotiate a week after signing a contract.

BW: I don't believe in that. I think it's pathetic.

The whole package amounted to about $10,000. At the time all of this conversation was taking place was in the spring of 1927. It was enough money, plus what Duke was providing me—I was doing some work, I had some jobs at Duke and that took care of a lot of things for me—this enabled me to get through college and not worry financially and enabled me, at the end of my junior year, to get married, which I did. And I'm still married to the same young lady; it'll be 65 years this coming September the sixteenth. And so everything's worked out nicely.

BK: Paul Krichell was quoted as saying you had the best baseball legs he ever saw, including Cobb.

BW: Well, I could run. I could run. I should've done a lot better in baseball than I did. Actually, in 1934 I kicked a water bucket and broke my big toe, and I didn't know that I had broken it. I played the last two weeks of the season with a broken great toe on my right foot. The next year I played the whole season with the aggravation of a broken toe. This is '35. I led the league in stolen bases on that broken foot, but it pained me the entire year. I had to have it operated on at the end of the '35 season. Dr. George Bennett of [Johns] Hopkins Hospital operated on it. Subsequently I had to have it operated on again as he told me would be necessary. This inhibited my ability to play up to the standards that I should've played and really made me more certain to get out of baseball than I was originally. That's my fault and not baseball's, but it was a good thing in a way because it made me study and it made me work in the wintertime and was a good thing on the whole.

BK: Your first full year in the majors was 1933; the Yankees sold you to the Red Sox. How did you feel?

Bill Werber (courtesy National Pastime).

BW: I didn't feel too good about that. I went to spring training in 1933 and I played practically all of the games at shortstop for the Yankees. In those games I fielded well and I hit about .350 and did very well indeed. In the meantime, Thomas Yawkey had bought the Red Sox; they had a scout over with the Yankees by the name of McAllister that was over there trying to buy some players to supplement what they had at the Red Sox. The Yankees had two other shortstops, [Frank] Crosetti and [Lyn] Lary, and when we broke spring training, [Joe] McCarthy took me out of shortstop—we went to Birmingham or Memphis and I don't remember which—but, in any event, he put Crosetti in to play shortstop and Frank did a good job. He looked good, hit good and then we moved on—I can't remember which cities we were playing, but we were coming north playing exhibition games—and Crosetti again looked good. As a consequence, McCarthy ended up selling me to Boston and keeping Crosetti. So I was very disappointed because I felt I had the job sewed up. But that was all right. You take what comes out. At the same time, Boston also bought Dusty Cooke, an outfielder, and George Pipgras, a pitcher. [Boston paid New York $100,000 for the three men.]

BK: You played with the A's in '37 and '38, then Connie Mack wouldn't give you a $1,500 raise and sold you to the Reds, where you got the raise. At the end of the year, you gave the raise back to the Reds. Why?

BW: There's a very interesting story connected with this. When I was over with the Red Sox, [Joe] Cronin [then the Washington manager] had made a disparaging, vulgar remark about the Red Sox in '33. I called him on it. I'm a little bit edgy about people making comments that I'm supposed to overhear *perhaps* and when he came out of the dugout I waited for him at third base and I called him on it. And he said, "Aw, Bill, I didn't mean anything—just adding impetus to the troops," or something like that. Anyhow, that was '33 when they [Washington] won the pennant.

So in 1934, when the season started, we opened in Washington. I got 4 for 4 on opening day. I got after Cronin and I stayed on him. I stayed on him the entire year of 1934 and made life pretty miserable for the fellow. Ultimately, when he came over in '35 to manage the Red Sox, I knew I would be traded and I did get traded to Connie Mack.

So I'm over with Connie Mack now and Pinky Higgins is playing third for the Rex Sox. Now I had a good year for Connie Mack [in '38] and felt like I was entitled to a minimum $1,500 raise and expected to get it. Mr. Mack was obdurate about the whole matter and the ballclub went off to Lake Charles, Louisiana, to train. I was working out of my father's office and doing very well. I had enough money that I made during the wintertime to take care of myself and my family and I was working out in the afternoons with the University of Maryland team—I lived not too far off of the University of Maryland campus—so ultimately Mr. Mack sold me to the Reds. This is just before both teams are about to break training camp; they're all through training camp just about.

So the first I heard about the sale was from an AP man whom I knew.

He said, "What are you going to do?" And I said, "Well, I don't know. I haven't heard from either ballclub."

So when Warren Giles of the Reds called and said, "We've acquired your contract from the A's. We'd like to have you show up in Tampa and we'd like to talk to you." I said, "Well, just put the $1,500 in my contract and I'll show up." And he said, "No we can't do that because we don't pay as much money in the National League as they do in the American." I said, "Well, Mr. Giles, that's too bad, because then I won't be there."

Then there was a lot of exchange of polite conversation and he said, "We're sorry. We'd like to have had you," and he hung up. Then came a call from Lake Charles, Louisiana, from Mr. Mack. "Why don't you go over and play with Cincinnati?" I said, "They don't want to pay me the $1,500 that you refused to give me." He said, "Well, make a deal for yourself." I said, "I'm not interested in that. I'm your property—*you* make the deal." And then this goes on and on.

He said, "You go over there and I'll send you a check for $1,500." I said, "No, I don't want your $1,500; I want it in a raise from the Reds. I want it in their contract." He said, "You'll have to work that out with them. Good-bye." "Good-bye, Mr. Mack." (Laughs)

So I finally get a call from Mr. Giles. He said, "I can't do anything till Bill McKechnie gets in. Bill McKechnie's been over to Miami to play an exhibition game." This that, this that. (Laughs) I said, "Fine. Call me when you make up your mind." He said, "Are you in shape to play ball?" I said, "Yes, I'm in shape to play ball."

And finally he called back and he said, "Come on down. We'll give you the $1,500."

At the end of the year we won the pennant. I think I made a significant contribution to help them win the pennant, so he calls me on the phone at my home in Cincinnati and says, "Bill, we've had a good year. You've made a big contribution. Could you stop in the office tomorrow? I'd like to sign you up before you go home."

I said, "Be delighted, Mr. Giles." And then I talked with Mrs. Werber and said, "What do you think we ought to get from him?" We talked about it and we decided what I was going to get. Now I get down to his office the next morning and he said, "What do you want to play for us next year?"

I said, "Mr. Giles, I don't know. You know more what I'm entitled to than I do. What do you want to give me?" And then he gave me a figure and I said, "That's $1,500 more than I had intended to get out of you. Last year you didn't raise too much of a fuss about the $1,500 I wanted and gave it to me, so this year I'll give it back to you." So I gave it back to him and he thanked me and took it.

BK: Go back a minute to Joe Cronin. How was he as a manager? Some didn't like him.

BW: I thought Joe was a good manager. He went out of his way to placate me. I found no fault with him at all. He was a good performer, he was a good battler, he was a good competitor. I'd rate Joe high on the list. I really would. I had no complaint over there at all.

You know, in connection with my holdout, a funny thing happened at the University of Maryland. It's an interesting story. Burton Shipley, the coach, and Miriam, his wife, were friendly with Tat, my wife, and myself, and I'd go up there and work out with the University of Maryland team. They'd have games between the varsity and the scrubs and I'd play third base for the scrubs. I'd have on an old raggedy pair of khaki pants and a lousy looking old, moth-eaten sweatshirt. The day that the varsity were issued their new uniforms—black caps and dark grey and gold uniforms, you know; they were handsome—they had a game and I played third base for the scrubs. That day I had about 3 for 4 and got an extra base on a single and stole a base and made some big league plays at third. The next day in the newspaper, the sportswriter that had been in the stands was highly critical of Burton Shipley, said that Ship never did know his ass from third base, or something to that effect, because the best ballplayer on the field was the scrub they had at third base. (Laughs) He said he couldn't figure out how they failed to issue me a uniform. (Laughs) He said, "The scrub playing third base was the best-looking ballplayer on the field."

BK: The only significant difference between the Reds of '38 and the Reds of '39 was you. Should you have been named MVP?

BW: I don't think so. As I remember, the '39 season we had [Bucky] Walters winning about 27 games and [Paul] Derringer winning about 25. Those two fellows won a hell of a mess of ballgames. Well, when you have guys that are winning like that and you have other fellows on the ballclub like Junior Thompson and John Vander Meer and Elmer Riddle and a real good staff that's coming in there and picking up slack, you got to give that pitching staff collectively more credit than any other individual.

And then you have Frank McCormick at first base that wakes up from his somnambulism and drives in 125 or 130 runs, or whatever he drives in, but he had a hell of a year. These things are related to each other and it's hard to say, but it wouldn't have been me.

BK: Talk about the '39 and '40 World Series.

BW: Well, since we lost the '39 World Series you'd naturally be disinclined to talk about it as much as you would about the second Series that you won. It's always nicer to be the World Champion.

In 1939, we had too many key players that failed to bat the ball out of the infield. I think that the Reds in '39 going into Yankee Stadium were maybe a little bit awed but we got nary a hit out of [Wally] Berger in left field, we got no hits out of [Lonny] Frey at second base, I don't think we got but one hit out of [Ernie] Lombardi in four games. The ballclub went into a general hitting slump. I don't think it was the Yankee pitching that did it so much as possibly the awe of getting into this World Series.

Now, Derringer, I do remember, in that opening game in Yankee Stadium pitched a 5-hit game and he should have won that game but [Charlie] Keller hit a fly ball to right-center that [Harry] Craft or [Ival] Goodman—either one—could've caught the ball, but they failed to call for it. Neither one called for it and the ball fell safely. Frey, the second baseman, could've gone out and caught the ball but nobody called for it. It's a thing that can happen but should never happen. But anyhow, Derringer, pitched superbly but lost the ballgame and that more or less set the key for the whole damn Series.

Then Lombardi got bowled over and knocked out by Keller in a game in Cincinnati which allowed [Joe] DiMaggio to run all the way 'round the bases and score and that was another tragic episode in the Series, so we lost that.

That had a salutary effect on the 1940 World Series because the team felt, when that World Series in '40 came up, that, by God, we were not going to be embarrassed a second time. That was the Series we were going to win come hell or high water. The general excellence of play was there and we beat a really good Detroit team in that 1940 World Series. It was a good Series and a lot of hitting on both sides and both Derringer and Walters, I think, won two games and both of them pitched very well.

BK: If you were allowed to run as they are today, how many stolen bases would you have had?

BW: That's a hypothetical question that really, with my mental makeup, I wouldn't be able to answer at all. The reason that I wouldn't is because the ballgame as played today by the individuals that play it and do the running is *entirely* different than the mental makeup in the individuals who were playing at the time that I played. To give you some interpretation: the only time that we ran were in those situations where the purpose of the running was to win the ballgame. Now today, that is not so. These fellows will run when they're 10 runs behind and they'll run when they're 10 runs ahead. That's for personal gratification or personal records, which the ballplayers of my day would not have taken into consideration at all. They just wouldn't have done it. As a matter of fact, they would have been subject to criticism by the other ballplayers on the club. "What are you trying to do, be a celebrity or something?" Your own players would have criticized you. It would not be justifiable. You stole when the purpose of the stealing was to *win* the ballgame or to put yourself into a scoring position where somebody making a base hit could help you win. It was different.

I don't know how many stolen bases but—hell, with Cincinnati you had Walters and Derringer pitching and in Cincinnati it's 110 and I'm on first base and we've got a two-run lead—not a hell of a lot of sense in me running and killing myself because they're not going to get two runs off Walters in two, three, or four innings anyhow. I mean, it just doesn't figure so you don't steal. I'm not out there trying to get medals. We've got the ballgame; we know it and the opposition knows it. They don't hit Walters anyhow, so you just don't run.

BK: Who was the best player you played with or against?

BW: I played with four ballclubs and I played with some of the best damn ballplayers that ever played in the American League. You'd have to go through and look at all these doggone names.

I'll tell you one durned good ballplayer in every way, shape, and form—you never hear anybody mention him—and that's Roger Cramer. Now Roger Cramer could do everything. He was a magnificent fielder, he was a good hitter, he was a good thrower, he was a good baserunner.

Now I played with [Jimmie] Foxx and Foxx stands up there in home runs, runs batted in, total hits—every criteria in the league, Foxx is right up there.

I loved Jimmie. Jimmie was a nice guy with a good disposition but, hell, on balls hit against the wall in Boston that I'd get two bases out of, he'd pull up at first out of breath. This doesn't help a ballclub.

Jimmie Foxx was a lovable guy. He was easy to get along with, nice fellow to have on the ballclub, never any difficulties. Strong as a bull. He could take one hand and put around one of my ankles and one around the other and lift me right up off the floor. We called him the Beast—he was that strong.

Frank McCormick was a hell of a ballplayer. He was a good fielder and he was a great hitter, but he was slow afoot.

Charlie Gehringer, was one of the best ballplayers that I ever played against. He was just about the perfect ballplayer: he was a good fielder, a smart ballplayer, great hitter, a good team player. He was a great ballplayer. Just great. Charlie was the kind of guy that continued to put fear in your heart, as a defensive player, when he had two strikes on him 'cause you knew he was going to swing once and when he swung he was going to hit the ball and he was going to hit it hard.

Going back to Jimmie Foxx, you know, he could run. In a hundred-yard dash in Boston in the latter part of the season, I got about a five-yard break on him and he beat me. There was a hundred dollar prize. I'd been fussing at him all year for never hustling.

Paul Waner—*hell* of a ballplayer! Great defensive player, great offensive player, great baserunner. Just couldn't get near him during August, though, when that heat came out—he smelled too bad with whiskey. (Laughs)

Course, I played against Rogers Hornsby. Now Roger was all through when I came up, but he played some for the St. Louis Browns. Ted Williams. Now Ted wasn't a good ballplayer, Ted was just a good hitter. Come right down to it, Ted was a sort of lousy ballplayer. You won't see many people that'll say that but that's the truth of the matter. He wasn't a good outfielder, he wasn't a good thrower, but he could wear that ball out—there wasn't any doubt about that!

Babe Ruth—the greatest of them all! If you look in the slugging averages in your *Baseball Encyclopedia* and measure his slugging averages with everybody else in there, there isn't anybody else close to him. *No*body! He was in the 800-percentile two or three times and there isn't anybody up in there. He was in the 700-percentile six, seven, eight times and, hell, Hank Aaron wasn't in there once.

Lou Gehrig—just a tremendous fellow. Just one of the greatest hustlers and greatest hitters and greatest competitors there ever was. There's a guy that played when he was hurt—played with a broken finger, middle finger on his glove hand. Just a magnificent ballplayer.

Wes Ferrell—no better competitor had *ever* been in the American League, and he belongs in the Hall of Fame. He has won more ballgames than Dizzy Dean. He was a better ballplayer. Wesley Ferrell was put into the outfield when your outfielders were hurt. Wesley was sent up to the plate to pinch-hit. Dean was never sent up to the plate to pinch-hit. That Wesley Ferrell, I think, has got more hits as a pinch hitter than any pitcher that was ever in the American League. Now I'm not certain about that statement but I think that's true.

And if the manager came out of the dugout when he was in trouble, he'd say, "Get your ass back in the dugout! I'm all right!" He didn't measure the number of balls he threw—whether he'd thrown 120 or 240—he didn't want to come out of there. He wanted to stay there until he'd won the ballgame, whether it was 12 innings or 15 innings or 22 innings. He didn't want to come out of there!

[Lefty] Grove was the same way. Those guys—they're fighters! Believe me. I wish all Americans were like those guys.

Now Grove had a minimal education but Grove on that mound was a lion! I'll tell you—the heart of a lion! And he came out of the mountains up there at Lonaconing in western Maryland and, boy, when you knew you had him out there, you had a Sergeant York! He was the type of guy, too, you better not come out there and ask him for that ball. (Laughs) He'd run your ass out of there! (Laughs) Those guys were characters. Nice fellows.

BK: Let me ask you about some players. Harlond Clift.

BW: There's a guy you never hear about but Harlond was a pretty damn good ballplayer. I don't know how you got his name here—you never see it in print—but he was a good ballplayer. I respected him. I thought he was a good ballplayer.

BK: Mel Harder.

BW: One of the smartest pitchers of his day. Mel Harder had a good fastball, a good curveball, a good sinkerball, and was *smart*. And he is a good citizen. He's a nice person, top flight. They've been promoting him for the Hall of Fame. Some man out there wrote me a letter and asked me a year or two ago to write a letter on his behalf and I looked up his record and wrote such a letter. It seemed to me at the time that he deserved consideration. Lot of people in there don't have the record that Mel Harder has.

BK: Bucky Walters.

BW: Bucky Walters was a pretty good third baseman but he was over at Boston and when I came over there Boston got rid of him and sold him to Philadelphia [Phillies]. And Jimmie Wilson made a pitcher out of him and he became an outstanding pitcher. Clean-living fellow, quiet, determined, never had much to say, never showed much emotion, just a real efficient workman. Mowed 'em down day after day after day. Nice fellow. I don't think he pitched long enough [to be considered for the Hall of Fame]. He was an infielder for a while and he stopped short, too. I don't think he had quite enough games under his belt. But a pretty good batter. In other words, when he was in the ballgame he could help the team by getting some hits himself.

BK: Ernie Lombardi.

BW: Only one guy was ever born like old Ernie. Big guy—about 6-4, 215, maybe a little bit more, I don't know. (Laughs) One of the greatest hitters that ever stepped up to that plate. He held the bat way down on the end with three fingers on the knob. He was quick to hit the ball. Didn't strike out much, but hit the ball hard. Good hitter. The greatest arm of any catcher I ever saw. Now they talk about Gabby Hartnett being a good thrower—he couldn't compare to Ernie Lombardi and neither could Bill Dickey. Neither could anybody I ever saw. And not only that, but Ernie Lombardi threw a very light ball. Some catchers throw a ball that, when it hits in your glove, you can feel it all the way up to your shoulder. Ernie threw a ball with a spin on it and when it dropped in your glove it felt light as a feather. Not only that, if a man was stealing third and Ernie dropped his arm, all you needed to do was put your glove down by the base and there was the ball, light as a feather, and if the man was sliding, the man was out. His arm was great. He's the only man that I've ever seen on wide throws reach out and grab the ball with his bare hand, you know, instead of quickly shifting over and catching with the glove backhanded. He'd just reach out with his bare hand and grab the ball and the ball would disappear. His hand was that big.

BK: Was he as slow as people say?

BW: Or slower. (Laughs) We all loved Ernie. Ernie was never out of sorts, good natured, decent. Nice, easygoing Italian fellow. Good to have on the ballclub.

BK: Arky Vaughan.

BW: I never had a word with Arky Vaughan. Arky Vaughan led the league [in hitting] one year, I know that, so he must have been a good hitter. You gain impressions about these people. I respected him as hitter but I never did much respect him as a shortstop. Now why I have that impression I don't know. But, anyway, I never did know him and am not able to make much of a comment on him. He just didn't impress you much.

BK: Is there a game or games that stand out in your memory?

BW: Well, I remember a game in Boston where I made four errors. The last error I made I went over behind second base and made a sensational stab with my outstretched gloved hand and turned around—did a sort of a little flip—and then I cut the ball loose and it went over the first baseman's head about 25 rows up into the stands. I can see that ball right now. It just went up in the stands about nine miles. In the inning after that, somebody hit a little pop fly to shortstop and I caught it. There was a pretty good crowd there and they all went, "Hooray!" And I'll never forget that ballgame because I always gave a maximum effort. There's nobody ever accused me of standing around with my thumb up my hiney. I was usually pretty active and aggressive and hustling. I said if the people can be so unkind—this is early on in my years at Boston—I said I don't think I'll ever pay much attention to fans in a ballpark again. I never did. I *never*, thereafter, ever let either praise or criticism from the press or the stands bother me either one way or the other. If it came one way or it came the other, it was all the same.

Then I remember a game in Cincinnati when we were playing the Cardinals and the standings were very close—they would win, we would win. They chased us the whole summer long. In this particular game, John

Mize would hit a home run and I'd come up and hit a double and John Mize would hit a home run and I'd come up and hit a double and tie the game up. I hit five doubles in that ballgame. We finally quit the ballgame in the thirteenth inning because both of us had to catch this train going east. They were going to Boston and we were going to New York. That was a memorable game because I hit those five doubles. John, I think, hit three home runs.

BK: You're the only person to have four doubles in a game in both leagues.

BW: That's right. I hit those four doubles off Mel Harder in Boston in 1935 and I hit the five doubles in that Cardinal game I was just talking about in '40.

BK: Do you still receive fan mail and do you sign autographs?

BW: I average—and it amazes me—about six or eight pieces of mail a week. The kids send 3 × 5 index cards, they send pictures to sign, and then a lot of time I get requests for pictures because they don't have any and I buy my pictures from (George) Brace in Chicago and I always honor these requests and write little notes. There is no charge for these things and I always answer the requests and notes.

BK: When this appears in print, the amount of fan mail will increase for a few weeks.

BW: It doesn't bother me. I'm retired. (Laughs) I've been retired for 22 years. I bought a home down here in Naples in January of 1972 and Mom and I've been living down here ever since.

BK: Tell me about the Jungle Club.

BW: When I got to Cincinnati—see, I didn't get down there until the day before they broke camp—I got down there on a Sunday and played seven innings against the Boston team. The next day spring training was over and we hit the road and started to come north.

Well, it didn't take me long to determine in my own mind that the ballclub was a little deadass. And, after a bit, when I got to know the guys in the infield a little better, I'd say, "Bounce around on the balls of your feet! Fire that ball!" I'd say, "Be a jungle cat!" And I'd fire that ball. I had a good arm; there wasn't anybody had a better arm anywhere and I could hang a clothesline out from third base and make that ball rise going across that infield. I don't mean to be bragging but I did have a good arm. I used to fire that ball and if that pitcher wasn't working I'd sometimes fire it at him.

Anyway, I'd fire that ball around and I got 'em to bouncing and I'd say, "Be a jungle cat!" And Frey had these liver spots all over his body—Lonny Frey—you know, part of his body'd be white and next to that'd be a big red spot. So I got to calling him the Leopard, because he was spotted all over. And then [Billy] Myers, the shortstop, says, "What are you gonna call me?" And I said, "We're gonna call you the Jaguar." And he says, "Who are you?" I said, "I'm the Tiger." And I gave him a growl and said, "Fire that ball!" And I got these guys fired up.

McCormick at first base, he says, "What am I?" I said, "You're a lead-ass." I said, "All you wanna do is to loaf. You hit. All you care about is hitting." McCormick would hit a ball to the infield and he'd figure he was out; he wouldn't run hard all the way to first base. If he'd hit a ball between the infield to the outfield, he wouldn't run hard to first base and take his turn so that he could end up at second if the outfielder would bobble the ball; and I'd get on his ass. I'd say, "Go down there as hard as you can and take your turn. That guy's gonna miss that ball out there in the outfield and you can end up at second base."

He said, "If I hustle good, will you take me into the Jungle Club?" I said, "We're not gonna promise you anything. You get out there and show us something!"

Well, he hustled. He started hitting and hustling. He said, "Take me into the Jungle Club." I said, "Buy us a beer and we'll do it." And he took us into the bar there at the hotel in Boston and we all had a beer. He said, "Am I in the Jungle Club?" And I said, "Yeah. You're in." He said, "What are you gonna name me?" I said, "You're the Hippopotamus." (Laughs) "No, no!" he said, "I don't wanna be the Hippopotamus!" And I said, "Okay, you're the Wildcat."

And he jumped off that stool; and ran out into the lobby there in the hotel and ran up to McKechnie and said, "They named me the Wildcat! I'm in the Jungle Club!" (Laughs)

And that's what the Jungle Club was. I helped infuse a little life into them and I think it improved their play in games.

BK: Do you recall on August 26, 1939, when you were the first player ever to bat in a televised game?

BW: I had no recollection of it at the time whatever. I didn't know about it after it was done. As a matter of fact, I didn't know about it until many years later. I didn't know about it until after I was retired and down here in Florida. One day I was passing the bag room of the club to which I belong and where I play golf—this is maybe 15, 16, 18 years ago. When I passed the bag room entrance, one of the bag room boys was reading a trivia book and he hailed me as I walked by. He asked, "Mr. Werber, did you know that you were the first player to ever appear in a televised major league ballgame?" I said, "No, I didn't know it." So he said, "Well, here it is right here in this book." And then he showed it to me and that's the first time I ever knew it at all. Since that time, I've read it in several different places and people have called it to my attention, but I didn't know it at the time.

BK: Do you have any regrets from your career and would you do it again?

BW: I have no regrets from having played baseball. I don't like the word "career." I never use the word. The players of my day never referred to it as careers. I never heard the expression used by players back then. They never viewed it as that. They were playing a game, they were having fun. I remember just like it was yesterday; I'm sitting in the dugout, Grove is going to pitch and I'm sitting on his left and Rick Ferrell is on my left and we're telling stories in the dugout. It's batting practice and we're laughing and giggling and Rick Ferrell nudges me in my ribs and we're all chuckling and laughing on the bench and he says, "Can you imagine getting paid for doing this?" And that's the way most of us felt.

Now those ballplayers in those days, they would not sign a contract for two or three years and you know why they wouldn't? Because they felt they were going to have a great year and they'd ask for more money the next year. I played 13 years and I never had more than a one-year contract—never *wanted* more than one year. I felt like I was going to have a hell of a year and next year I'd stick 'em!

Would I do it again? No, I don't think I would. I still think I was intended for the law. I never did get back to the law. I probably made more money by going the route that I did go. I did all of the necessary work to get a CLU degree and I became very successful in the pension business. When I turned my business over to my son, I had over a hundred pension cases on the books and I gave him that business.

The players were nicer then. It was a good bunch of boys. Those Cincinnati Reds and New York Giants—well, the Philadelphia A's had a lot of misbehaving—but most of the other teams, the boys were pretty solid. They were nice, clean-living kids—you know, the type of kids you could say, "Come on home and have dinner with us."

Most of the guys were lobby-sitters. You either sat in the lobby and talked baseball or went to the movies and that was the big deal. Mostly the guys 19, 20, and 21-years-old were married—nice girls, nice young men.

I enjoyed it. Some of the guys were not too well educated but they were nonetheless nice people. You don't have to be educated to be nice.

William Murray Werber

Born June 20, 1908, Berwyn, MD
Ht. 5′10″ Wt. 170 Batted and Threw Right

Year	Team	G	AB	R	H	2B	3B	HR	RBI	SB	BA	SA
1930	NYA	4	14	5	4	0	0	0	2	0	.286	.286
1933	NYA	3	2	0	0	0	0	0	0	0	.000	.000
	BosA	108	425	64	110	30	6	3	39	15	.259	.379
1934	BosA	152	623	129	200	41	10	11	67	40*	.321	.472
1935		124	462	84	118	30	3	14	61	29*	.255	.424
1936		145	535	89	147	29	6	10	67	23	.275	.407
1937	PhiA	128	493	85	144	31	4	7	70	35*	.292	.414
1938		134	499	92	129	22	7	11	69	19	.259	.397
1939	CinN	147	599	115*	173	35	5	5	57	15	.289	.389
1940		143	584	105	162	35	5	12	48	16	.277	.416
1941		109	418	56	100	9	2	4	46	14	.239	.299
1942	NYN	98	370	51	76	9	2	1	13	9	.205	.249
11 years		1295	5024	875	1363	271	50	78	539	215	.271	.392

**Led League*

World Series

Year	Team	G	AB	R	H	2B	3B	HR	RBI	SB	BA	SA
1939	CinN	4	16	1	4	0	0	0	2	0	.250	.250
1940		7	27	5	10	4	0	0	2	0	.370	.519
2 years		11	43	6	14	4	0	0	4	0	.326	.419

MONTE WEAVER

The Senators' Last Hurrah

1931–1939

The original Washington Senators existed for 60 years and more often than not the team was unsuccessful. It was often said that Washington was "First in war, first in peace, and last in the American League."

This was not totally true. The team actually finished in the cellar only ten times, but in 39 of its seasons in the nation's capital the Senators finished

***Above:* Monte Weaver (George Brace photo).**

good league back then, almost as good as the majors now, I think. I believe better than some [teams].

BK: Where did you go to college?

MW: Emory and Henry in Virginia, a small Methodist college in southwest Virginia. I went to the University of Virginia from there and did graduate work and taught there a couple of years.

BK: You have a Master's degree in math.

MW: I was on my way to getting a doctorate degree. I would have had it but I went to spring training instead. I didn't go back to teaching [after baseball] because I'd stayed out too long.

BK: After your rookie year, you dropped to ten wins.

MW: I hurt my shoulder pitching. I was out a couple of months. I never did get quite back to where I was before I hurt it. I finished up the '33 season when I got back to pitching. I think I won six games to help out winning the pennant.

BK: That was Washington's last championship team. You lost a heart-breaker in the World Series.

MW: Yes. I shouldn't have lost that one. We were going along, nothing to nothing, and Bill Terry came up. They put up temporary bleachers in right field—that was the short field. They wanted to seat more people. He hit a nice fly ball that just got into that temporary bleacher. That was a home run.

It went on to the eleventh inning and Travis Jackson, the third base-man, safely bunted down the third base line and they bunted him down to second base and Blondy Ryan hit a ground ball just through the infield and scored the run. If it hadn't been for the home run, I would have won it in nine.

BK: You were a pretty good hitter.

MW: Yes, I thought I was. I was always a pitcher in professional ball, but when I was younger playing sandlot ball I played shortstop. They needed a pitcher one day so they put me in to pitch and I never got back to shortstop again.

BK: Who was the best player in your day?

MW: There were several good ones. Charlie Gehringer was hard to beat. He was a great hitter and a good fielder. He didn't strike out much.

BK: Who was the toughest batter for you?

MW: Probably [Bill] Dickey was till I got acquainted with him a little bit more. He would take my fastball—I had a pretty good curveball—and he looked for the curveball and he could hit it. I soon found out that that's what he was doing and I quit throwing the curveball to him. He took three fastballs down the middle, knee-high, one day. He didn't swing. When he didn't swing he didn't take the bat off his back. He just stood there motionless and watched three go over. But he was a good hitter anyway.

BK: Who was the best pitcher?

MW: [Lefty] Grove was a great pitcher. He was consistently good. [George] Earnshaw was a great pitcher, but he wasn't as consistent as Grove.

I saw some of Bob Feller, too. He wasn't the great pitcher that he was later; he got better after I left the league.

BK: Your second baseman in Washington was Buddy Myer, an awfully good ballplayer. Does he belong in the Hall of Fame?

MW: I don't know. He would come pretty close. He was a good hitter and a real good fielder and a hustler. Some are in there who weren't as good.

BK: Is there one game that stands out, other than the Series game?

MW: We were working for a pennant in '33 and went into New York pretty much tied and we played a doubleheader. Earl Whitehill won the first game and I won the second game. That was kind of a top time to win a ball game. That's when Dickey took three strikes down the middle. Ruth and all were there and we beat them both games.

Earlier I won the first four games I pitched for Washington in '32 and I won one game the year before when I joined them, so I started off 5 and 0.

BK: You were in the major leagues through 1939.

MW: In '39, Washington sold me to Boston. They were trying to get players for the Louisville club. They had bought the Louisville club in the American Association. That's why they bought me. They couldn't get me out of the league on waivers until the middle of July. I found out later that the Yankees were claiming me. I hadn't pitched but ten innings and the Yankees came into Boston for Decoration Day, which was a big day in Boston, and I was the starting pitcher. I wondered about that. I beat the Yankees and I didn't start anymore.

What happened, George Weiss was the business manager in Baltimore when he sold me to Washington and he was the business manager of the Yankees then. I guess that's why he was claiming me.

BK: What is the biggest change in the game?

MW: Back when I was playing, we pitched nine innings usually. I don't know how come they don't keep them in longer.

I played a year at Durham, North Carolina, and I reported after I got out of the University of Virginia—the fifteenth of June. I started and completed 19 ball games up to September the sixth. I pitched all of them—I didn't get taken out.

George Whitted was my manager and after I pitched a couple of games

Monte Weaver (courtesy National Pastime).

after I joined them in June, I pitched a good game with two days' rest. He said to me afterwards, "I believe you pitch better with two days' rest. I'm gonna work you that way the rest of the year." And he did. I pitched a complete game every time. Sometimes they were seven-inning games because they didn't play on Sunday in Durham, so they'd play a doubleheader on Saturday—two seven-inning games.

Every fourth day I thought was the right amount. I didn't want more than that. Now they give them four days' rest—pitch them every five days. I don't think you can do as well that way. I came back after three days' rest.

One season when Walter Johnson was still pitching, they [the Senators] were playing the Yankees. They had a four-day trip but they were playing three games and he pitched all three games. He had one day of rest in between two of them. He shut them out three times. I don't know who could do that now. Of course, Johnson only won 400-and-some ball games. He had an easy motion.

What made Feller good, he had a good curveball and Johnson never did have a good curve. He didn't have much of a curve at all. His fastball, I'm sure, was alive. You know, it isn't the speed of a ball, it's what it does—whether it takes off or not.

BK: Do you receive fan mail today?

MW: Oh, yes. A lot of requests for autographs and pictures. I sign the autographs.

BK: Did you save souvenirs from your career?

MW: I've got some, not a great deal. I've got several books full of write-ups of games. I've got pictures of the '32 and '33 Washington clubs—mounted. Walter Johnson was the manager then [1932] and his picture's right in the middle of it. I'm proud of that one.

I didn't see him pitch, but he'd throw hitting practice and he still had a good fastball. His fastball would come in rising. He hit me in the knee one day when I was taking batting practice. It was black and blue in just a few minutes and I went into the clubhouse and put hot water on it to bring the color back in. Then I went out and pitched a ball game, beat the Athletics.

BK: Would you be a ballplayer again?

MW: Baseball was beneficial to me. I didn't play the first summer after I started college, but I played after that and paid my way through college with it. I didn't make much money, but it didn't take much. I was at Emory and Henry from '23 to '27 and it didn't cost me but about $450 [a year] in expenses. I made $300 a month over in Jenkins [Kentucky, pitching for a coal company team]—66 days for $660.

At the rate they're paying them now, I think I might try it today. You wouldn't have to be too good to get a good salary. I missed the pension. I was gone too soon.

BK: Do you have any regrets from your career?

MW: I guess you always wish you'd done better. That's about all.

I thought I'd probably go back to teaching earlier, but I didn't do that. After World War II I moved to Florida. I was in the service for three years over in Europe. When I came home I thought I would go to live in Washington—I had some apartments up there—but I didn't like Washington. It wasn't like the city was when I left it. Overcrowded and everything.

So I came down to Orlando and got into an awning business and then I got into the citrus business. I've been in the grove business; I guess I bought my first grove in '51. I've enjoyed it and my son took an interest in groves. He took courses in it in college and he'll inherit the groves.

Monte Morton (Prof) Weaver

Born June 15, 1906, Helton, NC
Died June 14, 1994, Orlando, FL
Ht. 6′ Wt. 170 Batted Left and Threw Right

Year	Team	G	IP	W	L	PCT	BB	SO	H	SHO	SV	ERA
1931	WasA	3	10	1	0	1.000	6	6	11	0	0	4.50
1932		43	234	22	10	.688	112	83	236	1	2	4.08
1933		23	152.1	10	5	.667	53	45	147	1	0	3.25
1934		31	204.2	11	15	.423	63	51	255	0	0	4.79
1935		5	12	1	1	.500	6	4	16	0	0	5.25
1936		26	91	6	4	.600	38	15	92	0	1	4.35
1937		30	188.2	12	9	.571	70	44	197	0	0	4.20
1938		31	139	7	6	.538	74	43	157	0	0	5.24
1939	BosA	9	20.1	1	0	1.000	13	6	26	0	1	6.64
9 years		201	1052	71	50	.587	435	297	1137	2	4	4.36
World Series												
1933	WasA	1	10.1	0	1	.000	4	3	11	0	0	1.74

ELDEN AUKER

Medicine's Loss

1933–1942

From 1907 through 1909, the Detroit Tigers won three American League pennants with a combination of excellent pitching and outstanding hitting. By 1911 the pitching was on the way out and the Tigers were sent into a two-decade period of mediocrity.

The hitting remained. First there was Ty Cobb and Sam Crawford, then Bobby Veach, Harry Heilmann, Charlie Gehringer, Dale Alexander, et al. As potent as these bats were, however, they had a hard time knocking in as many runs as the pitching allowed.

***Above:* Elden Auker (courtesy National Pastime).**

This is not to say the Tigers did not have any good pitchers during that period. Hooks Dauss was a top pitcher, as was Earl Whitehill, but Hooks was on the wane as Earl's star was rising. At no time could the team boast more than a couple of useful hurlers.

As 1930 approached, this began to change. Unnoticed and unheralded, Chief Hogsett joined the staff in 1929. In 1930 he was joined by Tommy Bridges, but still the team went nowhere. In fact, in 1931 only a Chicago team which still had not rebounded from the Black Sox scandal was between Detroit out of the cellar.

The next step came in December 1932 when longtime ace Whitehill was sent to Washington for Firpo Marberry and Carl Fischer. The Senators drew first blood in this swap; Whitehill had his only 20-win season in 1933 and led the Senators to the World Series, accounting for his team's only victory.

The rebuilding of Tigers staff was not yet complete. During the 1933 season, however, completion neared with the addition of two rookies. Schoolboy Rowe joined the team early, and then just after midseason Elden Auker was called up. The final touch was the acquisition via waivers of General Crowder in August of 1934.

The sticks were there: Gehringer, Hank Greenberg, Pete Fox, Goose Goslin, and Gee Walker. In 1934, 10 Tigers had 150 or more at bats and Fox was the weak link at .285. The team average was .300.

So the '34 Tigers reverted to the same combination the team had used so successfully a quarter of a century earlier—excellent pitching and outstanding hitting. And it worked. It worked again in 1935. Actually, it seems to be a nearly foolproof equation, with excellent pitching needed to be weighted heavier.

Elden Auker, the next-to-last addition to the pennant-winning formula, had been a three-sport star (baseball, basketball, football) at Kansas State University and had begun playing professional baseball only because he couldn't afford to go to medical school. He spent a lifetime being successful at everything he tried, so baseball's gain probably meant the loss of an outstanding member of the medical world.

In the two pennant-winning years of '34 and '35, Auker was a combined 33-14 (15-7 and 18-7) and his .702 winning percentage over the two years was the best in the American League. His .720 percentage in '35 led the league.

His ten-year major league record was 130-101. He retired at the peak of his game when he should have had three or four more good years left. In a recent interview he told of this decision and other aspects of his life, both in and out of baseball.

* * *

BK: You came to the Tigers in the 1933 season. What kind of minor league record did you have?

ELDEN AUKER: I couldn't tell you for sure. I was in the Texas League [at Beaumont] and I came up in July and I think I'd won 17 ballgames up to that time.

BK: So with the three wins in Detroit, you had a 20-win season. You must have been burning up the Texas League.

EA: Yes. I was doing real well.

BK: Was Beaumont the first place you played after you left college?

EA: No. I graduated from college on June the first [1932] and I'd signed with the Tigers and I went to Detroit the next day. I was in Detroit pitching batting practice for about a week before they sent me down to Decatur in the Three-I League.

I was down there for about four weeks—this was in the days of the Depression—and the league went broke. They sent Claude Passeau and me over to Moline of the Mississippi Valley League. We were there about six weeks and the season was all over.

The next year they sent me down to Beaumont. That was Class A in those days.

BK: A lot of guys went from Beaumont to Detroit.

EA: Yeah. There was Hank Greenberg and Schoolboy Rowe and that group. I came right up after them. I was only down there from the start of the season to July—only about two months, I guess.

BK: You played three sports in college. A football injury turned you into a submarine pitcher, is that right?

EA: Yes. I had my shoulder, in what they called in those days, "knocked down." Actually, it was a separation. I had it done twice. I had it done my sophomore year, my first year in football, and then I had it done later in my second year.

BK: Just couldn't bring the arm over the top anymore?

EA: No. I was muscle-bound and I couldn't get up over the top. I was throwing sidearm.

When I went down to Decatur, Bob Coleman, who was the manager down there, asked me if I ever tried to throw directly underhand. I said no, and he said there was a guy in the [National] league he used to catch by the name of Carl Mays. Coleman was quite a teacher in the minor leagues for the Tigers and he said, "You remind me a little bit of him. You're throwing sidearm and that plate's only 17 inches wide and you're throwing from sixty feet six inches. The tendency of sidearm pitchers is to be a little wild, have trouble getting it over the plate. If you get down right directly underneath, you could help your control a lot. Your fastball is good and if you could throw it down there you'd be much better off."

I pitched batting practice a couple of days and Quincy was coming to town. They were leading the league. He said, "I want you to start against Quincy. You're going to pitch nine innings—I don't give a damn if you walk everybody in the ballpark or what they do with you, but I want you to throw nine innings underhanded."

And I did. I walked one man and we won the ballgame one-to-nothing or two-to-nothing. I shut 'em out. They only got two hits off of me and from that day on I never threw any other way. I never had a sore arm or anything like that from it.

BK: In '34, your first full season with Detroit, you were a big factor in the Tigers' pennant. You won 15 and led the team in ERA.

EA: We had Schoolboy and Tommy [Bridges] and I just kind of fit into it as a starter. And we had Mickey Cochrane as our catcher and manager. He was a great catcher and he helped me considerably as a young pitcher.

The only thing we had on our minds was winning, winning. It wasn't so much of a thrill as it was just hard work. It became just a job, you know, after you once get in there and you get to be a part of the regular operation it becomes just another day's work.

BK: I talked with Billy Rogell, your shortstop, a while back and he says those '34 and '35 Tigers teams are generally overlooked when people talk of the great teams, but they were as good as any. What do you think?

EA: Yeah. In '34 we had, I think, our eight regulars all hitting .300 or right at it. Our infield drove in over 400 runs. If you couldn't win as a pitcher with them, you couldn't win at all.

I used to tell Charlie Gehringer the only way he got in the Hall of Fame was that I put him there. I said, "If I hadn't made any mistakes, you wouldn't have anything to do." (Laughs)

BK: In '35, you led the league in winning percentage.

EA: I think that was the year Schoolboy won 16 or 17 in a row.

BK: In '36 the whole team had a letdown.

EA: That was the year Cochrane got hit in the head. Bump Hadley hit Mickey in New York right in the first part of the year and that really upset a lot of things. He was the leader on the field and he was sorely missed, especially by the pitchers.

Schoolboy came up with a bad arm. We lost a lot of close ballgames. I lost a lot of one-run ballgames and we were shutout quite a lot.

Greenberg was out; he was missed and we just weren't clicking. When you lose a fellow like Cochrane, who was your manager and your leader, it's tough. We all had confidence in each other and we were really a close-knit group, and when they took him out it almost took the heart right out of us. I think we'd have won it again if he'd been in there and if Hank hadn't gotten hurt.

BK: You yourself came back pretty well in '37 but the team still finished second. Your 17-9 record may have been your best season considering your support. You had a lot of innings and a lot of complete games.

EA: I never followed those records until after I got out of baseball. In fact, I didn't know how many ballgames I won all together until I was out of baseball. (Laughs)

BK: Today, a man who wins 130 games in ten years is going to be paid about two million.

EA: Yeah, that's right. I think another figure that's more interesting today is the complete games. Some time ago, someone asked me a question about it and I looked it up. I pitched 126 complete games. That's something that's kind of unheard of today. There's only about three or four pitchers in either league that go out there to pitch nine innings.

When I came up to the Tigers, Mr. [Frank] Navin was the owner and he called me in the office the first day I got up there. He said, "Elden, I'd like to tell you a little bit of my philosophy. We're going to use you as one of our starting pitchers and I just wanted to tell you one thing: When you walk out on the pitcher's mound, we expect you to pitch the complete game, whether it's nine innings or ten innings or whatever it is. I can't pay two or three pitchers to pitch a ball game." (Laughs) "I can only afford to pay one pitcher."

BK: He's probably rolling in his grave today.

EA: (Laughs) That's the way we started out. We expected to pitch nine or ten.

BK: The kids today are only taught to pitch five or six. They can't go longer if they're not trained for it.

EA: I know it. That's the way the game has changed so much. They depend so much on relief. After they get by about the fifth inning, they start looking around for relief.

Your arm is like your legs. If you're going to run a mile, you've got to get your legs in condition to run that mile. You can't be a mile runner and only get your legs in condition to run a hundred-yard dash.

Another thing that has made a difference, which we didn't have, is the designated hitter. If we'd have had the designated hitter in our day, we could have pitched more complete games.

The World Series in 1935 against the Cubs, Bill Lee and I pitched against each other. He led the National League in pitching, I led the

American League. We left the ballgame for pinch hitters with the score tied two and two. We weren't knocked out of the ballgame, we were taken out for pinch hitters and that's what happened so many times in tough ballgames. When you get into a two-two or one-one ballgame and there's a man on base and it was your turn to bat, you expected to be taken out for a pinch hitter. Today you have some pitchers—guys like [Roger] Clemens and this guy [Jack] Morris—they go out there to pitch nine innings.

BK: After a good '37, you didn't pitch as much in '38—fewer games, fewer starts. What happened?

EA: Let's see. In '38—that was the year before I went to Boston. I didn't realize I started fewer games.

BK: Just looking at the record, it looks as if you may have missed maybe six weeks. Everything was down.

EA: Oh, wait a minute! Yes. I was out for three weeks with a broken foot. Luke Appling hit me in the foot with a line drive. I was on crutches for about two weeks. I forgot about that.

Also, Beau Bell hit me in the calf of the leg and severed the sciatic nerve that same year. I forgot all about those till right now. But I never had any arm trouble.

BK: How did it feel being traded to Boston after being with the Tigers for so long?

EA: I wasn't very happy about it, but we had a situation where Marvin Owen, our third baseman, was gone. Pinky Higgins was playing third base for the Red Sox and they had a young fellow named Jim Tabor that was burning up the minor leagues—a hard-hitting third baseman. Boston wanted pitching and Detroit needed a third baseman badly, so they traded me for Pinky Higgins.

It was all right about being traded—I didn't mind that—and I thought I'd just go ahead and pitch my ballgames, but when I got over there Joe Cronin was manager. Joe was a playing manager; he played shortstop. Joe was a very nervous individual. He was a guy that was running into the pitcher's mound about every other pitch and telling you what to pitch, "Keep the ball up, keep the ball down." His favorite saying was, "Don't give him anything good to hit, but don't walk him."

In the middle of the season, Tom Yawkey had Jimmie Foxx take over the pitching staff and handle 'em. We only had one guy on the pitching staff that knew what he was going to do or when he was going to pitch, and that was Lefty Grove. Lefty was a good friend of Yawkey so when he got ready to pitch, he just pitched. Cronin didn't know when he would pitch. When Lefty wanted to pitch, he'd just say, "I want to pitch today," and that was it.

Joe just had the whole pitching staff so screwed up, we never knew when we were going to pitch. I was working a ballgame against [Lefty] Gomez and the Yankees and we were in about the fourth inning and it was nothing to nothing or one to one—it was a tough ballgame. We were there in Boston, and Cronin had been to the mound about 15 times in the three innings. You know, when you're working a ballgame you're concentrating, just like it is when you're playing golf, and this guy was so distracting, not only to me but to the entire pitching staff. He also gave the signals to the catcher and was calling all the pitches.

We had Gene Desautels and a young catcher by the name of Johnny Peacock. When I was working with Mickey Cochrane, Mickey said, "Don't you ever throw a pitch that you don't want to throw. It's your ballgame and you're the guy that's got to get 'em out. I don't give a damn what I call for, if you don't want to throw it, don't throw it!" That's the way I worked with him.

When I got over to Boston, Cronin was giving the signals to the catcher whether it was going to be a fastball, curveball, screwball, or whatever. If I didn't want to throw a particular pitch I'd try to shake the catcher off and he wouldn't shake off. I didn't know what was going on until I was working with Desautels one game—a game against Mel Harder with Cleveland—and I shook him off a couple of times and he came right back with the same signal. Finally, I said, "What the hell's the matter with you? Why do you keep repeating these things? When I shake you off, I want to throw my pitch!"

He said, "Cronin's calling the pitches. You'll have to shake him off." I didn't know that up till then.

That was one of the things I wasn't used to and the constant running back and forth to the mound, too. One day I was working this ballgame against Gomez and he'd been out there all those times, when he came out the next time, before he had a chance to say anything, I said, "Joe, for Christ's sake, why don't you take the *&$%*# ball and pitch and I'll play short?!" (Laughs) I didn't pitch again for 21 days! (Laughs)

BK: In looking over your total career, that was your worst year.

EA: I requested to be traded that year. At the end of the season, Eddie Collins, who was the general manager, called me up and Yawkey was there and they wanted to talk about next year. I said, "Don't talk about next year, as far as I'm concerned, because you've just signed Joe Cronin to a five-year contract. There's no way I can do you any good. I cannot play ball for Joe Cronin! He's a nice guy and I have nothing against him personally, but I can't pitch for him and I can't win ballgames here for you. You either get rid of me or I'll retire." They asked if I was sure that was what I wanted to do and I told them that was exactly what I wanted to do.

So I got a call one day and it was from Fred Haney over at St. Louis. I knew Fred, he was a great guy. He said, "I have permission to talk to you. If we can buy you or trade for you, will you come over here and pitch for me?" I said, "I sure will!"

And I had three of the most enjoyable years of my career with Fred Haney. We didn't have much power. We didn't have guys like Greenberg and Gehringer and fellows like that. We had fellows that were real nice guys but we did *not* have much power on the ballclub and when you went out to pitch a ballgame, the joke used to be, if we got a run, they'd say, "There you are, Elden; go get 'em!" (Laughs)

BK: You had three solid years with a poor team.

EA: It was a different atmosphere. I was happy there. I was pitching my own ballgames and it was a different life altogether.

Mr. [Donald] Barnes, who owned the ballclub, was a terrific person and Fred Haney was a great manager. I thought a lot of him and we became very, very close friends. He and his wife, Florence, were great people. Even after we left baseball, we were very close to them. You know, you work better when you like the boss.

It was a little hot [in St. Louis], but we were very happy over there. That Sportsman's Park used to be just like a hot sandbox.

BK: You pitched the first night game in St. Louis history.

EA: Against Bobby Feller. He beat me by one run. He hit his home run off of me in that game—that's what beat me. He hit it in those little right-field stands out there. He hit a high pop fly out there. We've laughed about it afterwards.

I think the record will show that we each struck out, I think, 12 men and he struck me out 4 times and I struck him out 3 times (laughs) and then he hit that ball to right field.

BK: So he didn't outpitch you, he outhit you.

EA: (Laughs) The pitching was about equal, but the hitting was lopsided.

BK: You left baseball after the '42 season, when you had just turned 32 years old. Why?

EA: The war started.

When I was in college, I started out to be a doctor and I got all my premed work and got my B.S. degree but I didn't have any money to go to medical school, so I thought when I got into baseball I'd get enough money to go back to medical school. But I got married and we got into a couple of World Series and got caught up in the deal, so I began to kind of look around for something I might do after baseball and, through two or three friends of mine, I ended up getting in the abrasive business.

A friend of mine was the president of this small abrasive company. Abrasives—grinding wheels. So I got into that business in 1938, working in the winter time.

First I started down in the plant to learn what it was all about and then I went up and got in the sales engineering department. I was in there for a couple of winters.

Then, as the war came on, I started in the winter of 1940 working on antiaircraft guns—20 millimeter and 40 millimeter. The largest gun we had on aircraft up to World War II was a 75-caliber machine gun. The Germans were equipped with light cannon, so the 20 millimeter cannon became a very important piece of our equipment on the aircraft. That became a high priority.

Then the 40 millimeter guns were going on our ships that were taking troops around because the Germans were dive-bombing with these low-flying aircraft and the only thing we had for an antiaircraft gun was a three-inch gun and it was too big too handle for low-flying aircraft. So the 40 millimeter came in on pompoms so they could knock down these low-flying aircraft.

So the 20 millimeter and 40 millimeter became two of the highest priority items they had in the arsenal and I became an antiaircraft gun specialist during the war. During the '42 season, when we'd go to Washington, on my days off I'd go down to the Washington Navy Yard and work with them. In the winter I was spending all my time down there.

Mickey Cochrane had gone over to Great Lakes [Naval Station] and he wanted me to come over there with him and they wanted to put me in as a Lieutenant Junior Grade. I was married and had a son and was not eligible for the draft, but in the winter of 1942 the government came out with an edict and froze me on this job on antiaircraft guns. So all during the war I worked on those darned antiaircraft guns. I worked with 27 gun arsenals over the United States and Canada and that's all I was doing.

Then, after the war was over, I continued with the [abrasives] company and became vice president in charge of sales and then another company came along and wanted me and I'd been having a little bit of a problem with the guy that was the president. He wasn't treating some of the people just right, I didn't think, and I went with the other company.

To make a long story short, I went there as sales manager for 'em and I was with 'em for 25 years and I became vice president of marketing and then president of the company the last eight years I was there. We had grown into the second largest in the industry and became a division of Dresser Industries. I was also vice president of Dresser. I retired as president in 1974 and went to Washington for a year for the corporation.

BK: You've been pretty successful at everything you've done.

EA: I've been pretty lucky. I've been most fortunate and I'm very grateful to whoever causes all these things. I also had a good partner. I picked her up in 1933. That helps.

I've been very happy and now I'm happily retired down here. I've been playing golf two or three times a week. I had a pacemaker put in a few years ago and it's keeping me going.

At 80 years of age I shot a 76 on the golf course. (Laughs) I shot my age, so I've done something Nicklaus and Palmer haven't done. (Laughs)

BK: Who was the best player you saw during your playing days?

EA: I think the best all-around player in the American League—that's where I spent my time—was Charlie Gehringer. Best day-in and day-out, year-in and year-out. He was a great ballplayer—great hitter and fantastic fielder and just like a mechanical man. On top of that, he was a great person. We had a lot of great ballplayers in those days, of course. Babe Ruth was just finishing up, but he was still a wonderful ballplayer.

BK: Who was the best pure hitter?

EA: I think Ted Williams was. I was with Ted his first year up in 1939. I played with him for one year and pitched against him for three years and I was always thankful I didn't have to pitch against him four years. (Laughs) He was a real *pure* hitter. And they said Ruth could just about hit at will.

DiMaggio was a great hitter. I was lucky—Joe didn't like my style of pitching much. We were very good friends and we used to have a lot of fun back and forth about it.

I had his streak stopped in New York up to his last time at bat, and he hit a ball down to Harlond Clift at third base. They could have either given it a hit or an error and they gave him a hit on it. I think anything that was close in New York they gave him the benefit of the doubt. It had to be a pop fly not to be a base hit. (Laughs)

Joe was a hell of a hitter and a great ballplayer—one of the greatest arms I ever saw.

The thing about Ted Williams, also, he didn't really get the credit for being the outfielder, but he was a hell of an outfielder. He was a guy a little bit like Charlie Gehringer—he seemed to sense where to play. When the ball was hit to left field he wasn't too far to the left or too far over to center. It seemed like he was always near the ball. He studied those hitters as much as he did the pitchers, and he had a great sense for being close to the right place most of the time.

On top of that, he took long strides and he got a break on the ball and he was always in the ballgame. He didn't have his head up in the stands looking around.

When I was with him his first year up he didn't smoke or drink—that's the kind of guy he was when he came to the Red Sox. He saved every penny he had and sent it home to his mother, who worked for the Salvation Army. He said, "First thing I'm going to do is make her independent for life, and then whatever money's left over I'll take." That's something a lot of people don't know about Ted Williams 'cause he wouldn't tell you.

He's really a great guy. Mrs. Auker said his biggest thrill was to come out to our house and eat fried chicken and drink Coca Cola. (Laughs) He loved that.

BK: Who was the best pitcher you saw?

EA: Lefty Grove was just finishing up, but when I first came up Lefty was really awesome. Then I would say the young guy that came up was Bobby Feller. He was probably the toughest guy that I've seen out on the mound over the years.

They had another pitcher on the Cleveland ballclub that was a good pitcher, Mel Harder. People don't ever take into consideration that he was a good pitcher, but he was a great pitcher.

BK: I agree with you. Considering his pitching record and his contributions as a coach, he belongs in the Hall of Fame. I interviewed him several months ago.

EA: Is he still alive? If you ever speak to him, tell him I send my love. We were good friends. Mel and I used to really get tied up in some pitchers' battles, but he was a real gentleman. He was a fine person.

Other pitchers we had in those days were Red Ruffing and Lefty Gomez of the Yankees. There were a lot of good pitchers in those days—Teddy Lyons over with the White Sox, [Rube] Walberg, Monte Pearson, Schoolboy Rowe, Tommy Bridges.

Bridges and I were roommates. He was a great guy—had a heart like a lion.

BK: You and he were both pretty good hitting pitchers.

EA: That Gomez still owes me a twenty dollar hat. I told him I'd outhit him a hundred points. (Laughs) And I did and he never did pay me! Gomez loved to hit but he didn't get too many hits.

BK: Is there one thing that stands out most in your career?

EA: Oh, golly. The World Series, of course, you'd think was a thrill—and it was!—but I really don't have any single thing. I guess maybe I'd say in '34 when I beat the Cardinals in the World Series. I was young and it was early in my career.

Just being on a winning ballclub and winning a pennant was a great thing. I didn't think so much about a thrill to myself as the thrill just to be with a winner.

I think it was in 1935 I pitched a game on my birthday against the St. Louis Browns and beat 'em two to nothing, I believe. I beat Ivy Andrews, as I recall. That cinched the pennant for us.

BK: I guess it's easier to look back and see what was a thrill than to think about it at the time.

EA: You're right. When you're in a situation—when it's your business—you don't think about things being such a thrill because you're on the team with a bunch of guys out there all striving to do only one thing and that's win the ballgame. If you win, that's great and you share in that joy. Maybe there were times something thrilling happened to me and we lost the ballgame and I forgot what the thrill was.

BK: It doesn't seem that that team orientation is quite the same today.

EA: I don't see how it can be with all the differences in the salaries and the way the whole attitude has changed.

I think probably one of my greatest thrills, if I was really going to look at a thrill, was the day in the 1935 World Series when Goose Goslin got the hit that drove in Mickey Cochrane that won us the World Championship and I was sitting on the bench when that happened.

What was interesting was when that inning started, Goose Goslin and I were sitting on the bench. I remember it like it happened yesterday. I was sitting there on the steps and he came over and sat down beside me and he said, "You know, I've got a hunch. I'm going to be up there with the winning man on base and if I am, we're going to win this championship."

He had about three guys ahead of him before he even came to bat. Mickey got on base and got over to second base and there were two men out. Goose came to bat and got that hit into right field to win the Series.

He came back after it was all over and threw his arms around me and said, "What'd I tell you! What'd I tell you!"

That was thrilling. We were all young kids and here we were in the World Championship. Three years prior to that I was worrying about whether I was going to pass my grades in college or even graduate. (Laughs)

Getting an education is the most important thing in the world because you never know what's going to happen in that game. You can be there a year or two years, five years, ten—you never know. All at once, one day you wake up and it's all over with.

BK: You mentioned a couple of changes—salary and the designated hitter. What do you think the single biggest change has been in the 60 years since you started playing?

EA: If I was going to name the single biggest change, I think it would be in the ownership of the teams. That may sound a little bit far-fetched,

Elden Auker (courtesy Detroit Tigers).

but I think this is what's happened in baseball—you have businessmen today involved in baseball that know very little about baseball. They're very wealthy, they've made their money in something else and—I don't know 'em personally—it seems to me that so many of 'em are just on ego trips.

When I played in the American League we had eight teams. We had

Mr. Navin, who was a dedicated baseball man—that's all he ever knew—and he was president and major owner of the Tigers until he died in 1935; Lou Comiskey in Chicago; Mr. [Clark] Griffith in Washington; Connie Mack in Philadelphia; [Jacob] Ruppert in New York, who was a beer man. However he had an organization that was baseball; he wasn't in there for any ego trip. He had people running it that really knew what was going on.

In those days, also, there was the family in St. Louis that was there for years and years. I can't recall their names now, but it was a baseball family. In Boston was Tom Yawkey, another dedicated baseball man. Cleveland was owned by the guy that owned the Nickel Plate Railroad—he was a baseball man. I don't recall his name. All of them were baseball men.

You had [Charles] Stoneham in New York and [Philip] Wrigley in Chicago and the Robinsons in Brooklyn. They were owned by baseball people; they weren't owned by pizza parlor owners and hamburger kings and corporations and things like that.

I think that what has happened, the management that they have hired is not baseball. The Dodgers train down here in the spring and Ben Wade, who just retired, I've known ever since he was a kid. His brother Jake and I were in the minor leagues together and he went with me in the trade to Boston.

I saw Ben one spring. I usually go out and spend a little time talking with Tommy Lasorda and Ben—they're about the only ones that are old enough so we can talk about anything. I was talking with Ben when they had this [1981] baseball strike on and I asked him, "What's this thing all about?"

He said, "It's a deep-seated problem. We have a bunch of owners in baseball and very few of 'em are baseball people. I'm fortunate enough to be with one organization with Mr. [Peter] O'Malley, who happens to be a dedicated baseball man. That's all he's ever done. His dad was a lawyer, but baseball is all Pete knows.

"And," he said, "did you know that in 26 teams in the major leagues, myself and two others that are the head scouts are the only three that have ever played professional baseball? The rest of them are parts of the family, friends, buddies, and so on."

As one little example, look in Detroit with [Tom] Monaghan. Who'd he hire to head up his ballclub? A football coach.

This is what I think you have that has changed the whole aspect of the game. Now this starts and then its comes up with the player himself.

When I went to the Tigers I talked personally with Mr. Navin. When I walked into Navin Field that first day, there was a message for me to come up to talk to Mr. Navin. And that was the process—every one on that ballclub had Mr. Navin *personally* involved with them. He knew us, he knew where we came from, he knew what kind of people we were and we knew what kind of a guy he was. Today, the ballplayer has an agent and the owners have guys in positions that can't cope with these things. It's gotten away from them, with salaries, for example.

And then along comes a union. The union is a natural thing. They tried to organize us back in 1934. We had people come in to talk to us and we ran 'em out of the clubhouse. We didn't even let 'em *into* the clubhouse. It was ridiculous, we didn't want any union. Course, that was in the days in Detroit when we were very conscious of unions 'cause they were having a lot of trouble in the automotive industry.

When you've got a problem between the employee and the employer, you usually end up with a union and this is what has happened in baseball. As a result, now you have the players and the union that are running the owners and the owners are looking around and can't figure out what's happened. They try to blame the ballplayers and that's a natural thing to do, but they're the ones that let it get away from them.

It's like any other business and I was in business for years—we didn't have a union because we had good management. The way you keep a union out is with good management. Once your unions get in, they're going to call the shots, 'cause that's what that head of the union is for—that's how he makes his living.

Can you imagine what would happen if Judge Landis was alive and some guy came out to the ballpark full of drugs? We were afraid even to go to the racetrack on an off day—afraid Landis would hear about it.

On Thursday before [former commissioner A. Bartlett] Giamatti died on Saturday—I had met Dr. Giamatti down here in Vero Beach and spent a little time talking to him—I wrote him a letter and I said I thought he had a great opportunity to really do a service to this country and especially to baseball. I said I would like to make a suggestion.

I said baseball has been fooling around too long with drugs for several years and not getting anyplace. I said I'd like to see professional baseball take the leadership in this thing 'cause we've got millions of kids all over the United States that are looking to the professional baseball players as heroes. It's been that way long before I started playing, they were that way when I was playing.

I recommended that professional baseball take the leadership and establish a firm policy that any professional baseball player—in the minor leagues or the major leagues—that is ever convicted of using any illegal drugs be automatically suspended for one year and during that year he would receive no pay and he would have to pay for his own rehabilitation.

The ballclub, the league, the union, or anyone else could not subsidize the treatment in any way. If he came back and was convicted a second time, he'd be banned for life.

And, also, any professional baseball player that was convicted of transporting or selling drugs would be suspended from baseball for life on the first conviction. It's a very simple rule and would be very simple to enforce and that would put professional baseball on a level it does not enjoy today.

Dr. Giamatti died probably before he ever read the letter. I never heard from [Fay] Vincent.

When I was in Washington, and being from Kansas, I know Senator [Robert] Dole pretty well, so I sent him a copy of this letter. I said I would like to recommend, if the president of the United States is serious about this drug business and is worried about the kids, that this policy be put in for all professional athletics. Throughout the country, you've got kids that worship the professional athletes and, if the United States would take this very simple policy and put it into effect, we could clean up all of our sports so we wouldn't have the problems we have with guys like [Ben] Johnson in track. Sports would be absolutely clean of drugs.

This would be far-reaching. It would go back down to the colleges, it would go to the high schools, it would go to the grade schools. All of these kids that aspire to be professional athletes, if they kew their sport was *absolutely* free you'd see a great change in the attitude of the young people.

I got a little note from Dole. He said, "Thank you and I'll pass it on." I never heard anything.

So I wrote William Bennett. I heard him one night and he said something about sports and I also wrote to Jack Anderson, the columnist, because I heard him talk one night about the kids in America that were watching the athletes and he thought it was a shame. I've never received a reply from either of them.

I know the unions would fight it and I know the owners would fight it. The owners would fight it because they have an investment.

I saw a cartoon a couple of years ago. It showed a building with "Drug Rehabilitation Center" on it and three little kids standing outside at it and the caption was, "Waiting for their heroes to return." That was one of the saddest cartoons I ever saw in a paper.

The business world is a little different. I'll tell you this, as president of my company, if I ever found that I had one of my men—either one of my executives or anyone in an important position in the company—using drugs, I don't care who he was or how long he'd been with the company, he'd be gone. Now. There'd be no fooling around. I did that with guys who drank. I'm not a teetotaler, but I couldn't put up with drinking. You can't be lenient—it just compounds the problem. They take advantage.

It's like this Pete Rose deal. They're put in the Hall of Fame by sportswriters—they can't do anything about that. There's no doubt that he's not suitable, but there's a lot of sportswriters that will try to bend that thing and get him in there.

I will say this: I'll never be in the Hall of Fame, but if they're going to put guys in there like Pete Rose, I don't want to be in it. When you've got a guy like Charlie Gehringer in there and then to put Pete Rose in there beside him, it makes me sick to think about it.

BK: Did you save souvenirs during your playing days?

EA: Oh, no. I have a few baseballs around and I've got some pictures and scrapbooks. I never kept a scrapbook myself but I had fans that would send 'em to me. They would keep them and as the year ended, they'd send 'em to me. I have quite a few around.

BK: Do you receive much fan mail today?

EA: Oh, yeah! I get eight, ten, twelve letters a week. They're from autograph collectors. I get 'em from people that say they used to see me pitch. Some come from people that are retired and are baseball fans and they are quite serious with their collections, particularly with certain teams like Detroit. I get letters from a lot of fans in Detroit, and from all over the country, really. Then there's the youngsters that have never seen me and don't know anything about me, but they say their grandfather told them about me. (Laughs)

I had an interesting one happen this past winter. I got a call from a fellow from Detroit and he said he was coming to Florida and he wanted to know if he could stop by and talk to me. He had a bat and some baseballs that he wanted me to sign. He said he was a Tiger fan and he saw me pitch my first ball game in Detroit.

I didn't think too much about it and one day I received a telephone call and he was over in Lakeland. His name was Elmer Kapp and he said that he and his wife were there and he wanted to know if he could come over and get my autograph. When he got here, he was blind and he'd been blind since he was a young man, but when he could still see he saw me pitch my first game. He said he followed me all through my baseball career. I felt flattered.

BK: If you were to go back to Kansas State, would you do it all again?

EA: Well, if I'd had the money, I hoped to have been a doctor.

I did receive a call the other day, which was highly flattering, from a fellow by the name of Nelson from Kansas State University and he said that he was chairman of the Kansas State University Hall of Fame, which they'd just started up. He wanted to tell me that I was the first one to be elected and wanted to know if Mrs. Auker and I could come out to be inducted. That's an honor.

In 1969, I think it was, I was inducted into the Hall of Fame of Kansas. I was the twenty-seventh member. Walter Johnson is one of them that's in there; that's pretty good company. (Laughs)

BK: Were you satisfied with your baseball career?

EA: I kind of wished I could have played another couple of years because I quit when I was on top, I guess you'd want to say.

I enjoyed it, but, on the other hand, it was probably a break that I got out of it because if I'd stayed around I'd have been like a lot of others. I wasn't interested in staying in the game as a manager or coach or anything like that, and I wanted to get into business and I had an opportunity to do it. I had to make the decision whether I was going to play the '43 season or get out of it.

I got a call from Clark Griffith when I said I was going to retire. He said he'd talked to the president of the United States and he was calling the ballplayers and trying to get 'em to play because it was going to keep up the spirit of the country and keep baseball going. He thought that I was kind of letting 'em down by not staying in the game.

I didn't want to quit, but I had an opportunity. It wasn't much of a financial opportunity. (Laughs) I left the game making twenty-seven five and took a job for 500 a month. (Laughs) In the long run, it turned out to be a pretty good decision.

I was getting to the point where those line drives were getting back through that box a little bit quicker. I wasn't as agile as I used to be. (Laughs)

Elden LeRoy (Big Six) Auker

Born September 21, 1910, Norcatur, KS
Ht. 6′2″ Wt. 194 Batted and Threw Right

Year	Team	G	IP	W	L	PCT	BB	SO	H	SHO	SV	ERA
1933	DetA	15	55	3	3	.500	25	17	83	1	0	5.24
1934		43	205	15	7	.682	56	86	234	2	1	3.42
1935		36	195	18	7	.720*	61	63	213	2	0	3.83
1936		35	215.1	13	16	.448	83	66	263	2	0	4.89
1937		39	252.2	17	9	.654	97	73	250	1	1	3.88
1938		27	160.2	11	10	.524	56	46	184	1	0	5.27
1939	BosA	31	151	9	10	.474	61	43	183	1	0	5.36

Year	Team	G	IP	W	L	PCT	BB	SO	H	SHO	SV	ERA
1940	StLA	38	263.2	16	11	.593	96	78	299	2	0	3.96
1941		34	216	14	15	.483	85	60	268	0	0	5.50
1942		35	249	14	13	.519	86	62	273*	2	0	4.08
10 years		333	1963.1	130	101	.563	706	594	2230	14	2	4.42

**Led League*

World Series

Year	Team	G	IP	W	L	PCT	BB	SO	H	SHO	SV	ERA
1934	DetA	2	11.1	1	1	.500	5	2	16	0	0	5.56
1935		1	6	0	0	.000	2	1	6	0	0	3.00
2 years		3	17.1	1	1	.500	7	3	22	0	0	4.67

FLEA CLIFTON

Cobb's Disciple

1934–1937

You are the manager. You have just led your team to its second straight league title. Last year you were favored to win the World Series but lost

Above: **Flea Clifton (courtesy Flea Clifton).**

in seven games. Some say your team is not as good as it looks, but this year, even with a poorer record, you are still on top.

This year your Series opponent is favored. You split the first two games, played in your ballpark, and your opposing manager says he was looking for a split there. And your second game was costly: you lost your first baseman. He is out for the remainder of the Series with a broken wrist.

This is not just *any* first baseman, however; this is the most potent offensive force in the game. He has driven in more than 300 runs the last two seasons, 170 this year alone. And he plays every day, so you have no backup.

Your third baseman originally signed as a first baseman, though he has not played the position in four years. You put him there and hope it all comes back to him. This, of course, now leaves you with no third baseman, but that is not much of a problem because on the bench is a young man in his second major league season who is ready to play. He is always ready to play, but with your starting infield there just is not much playing time available—those guys play *every* day.

You put the kid in. You have, in essence, just substituted your *least* powerful batter for your most powerful. But it works. You win your club's first-ever World Championship, 4 games to 2.

Your name is Mickey Cochrane and your team is the 1935 Detroit Tigers. The kid's name is Herman "Flea" Clifton, and if you look at the Series' summary it looks as if Flea did not contribute a lot. The scorers, though, were unkind to him. He was given an error in the field on what should have been a hit, and he was robbed of a hit when the scorer called a very difficult chance an error.

This play, however, swung the Series solidly to the Tigers. Detroit was up, 2 games to 1, in Chicago and General Crowder was pitching against Tex Carleton. Tied 1–1 in the sixth, Clifton hit a fly over the head of Cubs' left fielder Augie Galan. Galan went back for the ball, but it tipped off the end of his glove. Clifton never broke stride and ended up on second base. Crowder, the next batter, hit a ground ball which shortstop Billy Jurges bobbled and the speedy Flea scored all the way from second. Crowder made that run stand up, ending with a five-hit, 2–1 victory and giving Detroit a 3–1 edge in games.

Flea Clifton did not have a long major league stay—four years—and with an infield of Greenberg, Gehringer, Rogell, and Owen ahead of him, playing time for reserve infielders was limited. His boyhood dream, though, was to play for the Tigers and he did it.

* * *

FLEA CLIFTON: I only had one desire—that was to play for Detroit. Coming up behind a guy like Gehringer is pretty tough competition and my roommate, Billy Rogell, was one hell of a shortstop and that infield as a whole was terrific, so you just made the best of it.

On our team there's only five of us left now. A few years back I tried to get each one of 'em to put a hundred bucks up a man and the last man left would get the pot and they said, "Hell no! You'd live the longest of all of us just to get the pot!" (Laughs) I said, "You're right!"

I was the baby, the youngest member on that ballclub. I guess the guys that kept it clean all their life are still around. The ones that enjoyed themselves as they went along, why, I guess they're gone.

I went to the college of hard knocks. I could've gone but I got into professional baseball. The fact is, at the time I was going to Ludlow High School [in Kentucky] and I went back to see my history teacher. I was an orphan; I didn't have anybody to explain things and I had scholarships, football scholarships—Purdue and Dayton and Iowa—and the only one I could talk to was her. I went back to see her and she said, "Take your baseball 'cause you'll make it." And she was right. My life's ambition was to play at Detroit and I made it.

There was one guy that put me there, and that was Ty Cobb. I got his book when I was a kid and he turned out to be my guiding light. Unfortunately, he's the one thing I missed. He was gone about two years before I got there, and I'm sorry I missed him.

He got bad press from some of those guys. I got this from Dan Howley, who was very close to him. He was very opinionated and a dedicated man and the press was unkind at times, so he didn't get the press although he stood head and shoulders above anything that came along at that time, or *this* time, for that matter. [Howley had been a coach with Detroit when Cobb was the team's manager.]

But I think the two of us were of a temperament, and he was the guiding light for me. He kept me out of a lot of trouble. That was worth everything. I'd try to do everything Ty Cobb did, but I was 5-foot-11 and 160 pounds and he was 6-foot-1 and 190 pounds. But I'm not too sure he could've outrun me. I would've enjoyed meeting him, just to shake his hand and thank him. I still have his book, too, and I'm trying to get a grandson now to read it.

I turned down more money to sign with the Cardinals to sign with Detroit because of Ty Cobb. He was the reason I wanted to play for Detroit.

Billy Doyle was the [Tigers] scout. The National Baseball Federation tournament that year was held in West Baden, Indiana, and we won it and I was picked as the shortstop for the tournament and Billy came down and started talking to me. Of course, he didn't have to talk to me; he was from Detroit and my mind was made up to play with Detroit. It was my lifetime ambition.

BK: After they signed you, you were sent to Raleigh [Piedmont League] and you met up with Hank Greenberg.

FC: Hank and I started at Raleigh, then the group joined up in Beaumont [Texas League] and then from there a batch of us went from Beaumont to Detroit. Must've been ten of us. If they get one player today you'd think they've really done something. There was a batch of us that went up there from Beaumont.

I was two years at Beaumont. The first year I was the Texas League [all-star] shortstop and the second year they did me a big favor. They decided they wanted me to play second base, so they put me there and I wound up being the all-star second baseman.

That was like Uncle Remus when they put me at second base—"Don't throw me in that briar patch!" Second base is probably the most important infielder out there, and you have an *instinct* for it 'cause you've got two bases to cover and so forth. You have to know which base to cover and when. Of course, you're making that double play, too.

In '32 I hurt my leg sliding and dislocated the right knee. It didn't break, it just slipped outta socket. Del Baker was the manager down there and I was runnin', hobblin', because we were gonna play the all-star game and I wanted to play in that.

But they were right and I was wrong. They kept me out and, although I was hobblin' and runnin' every day, Del Baker would come in every inning and I was giving him hell, tellin' him I was ready to play. Finally, he looked at me and he said, "Damn it, you're worse than a sand flea!" Tom Holly was sittin' there; he said to Tom, "Why don't you give him a chew of tobacco and shut him up? He's drivin' me nuts!" Well, Tom gave me a chew and I've been chewin' ever since.

We had that big righthanded pitcher, [Schoolboy] Rowe, and there was another one should've come up but he was somewhat of a playboy—outfielder by the name of Taulbee—but he never made it because he had fun on his mind. But he was as good an outfielder as you wanted.

I was the baby over at Raleigh. Greenberg and I were the only ones there to make it [to the majors]. They moved Hank and I to Beaumont, but Hank came up a year before I did. He came up in '33 and then I came up in '34.

It wasn't a very enviable position. Billy Rogell, my roommate—he's in

Florida now—sent me some cards that showed the record for that infield. For '34 and '35, they averaged out 100 RBIs for two straight years! Lord knows what that infield would be worth today.

There wasn't anybody that'd have a chance to break in on that infield, but I practiced every day just like I was gonna play in every game. And Mickey even put shin guards on his infielders so nobody got hurt. He figured that they signed a contract, and they were supposed to be the regulars, and the team was goin' good. They played. That was it. Nobody else played.

Come time for the '35 World Series, after Hank got hurt he had two veteran infielders on the club. I went to Hank's locker and picked up his glove. Hank asked what I was doing and I told him I would play first base. That's when Mike sent word that I was gonna play third and Owen first. Before that he had said [Heinie] Schuble would play. Somebody asked him, "Why did you put that rookie in there?" He said, "That was easy! He's a winner!" And that's the way it turned out.

Mickey, when he put me at third base, he knew what he was doin' because then he had two shortstops on the left side of the infield and there wasn't anything goin' through there with Rogell and I on that left side. I gave him what he wanted and that was defense. He knew these other guys that were older and more experienced than I was; he figured that they wouldn't cover the ground that I would cover out there.

Mike didn't miss a trick, you know—how the guys deploy themselves even if they weren't playing. He knew damn well if he put me in that ball game I was in shape and I was ready to play. And he was right. I had the desire. I think I had about 14 times at bat and I hit 7 or 8 line drives that were caught. I hit it over his [Augie Galan's] head and he was runnin' with his back to the infield and the ball hit on the tip of his glove and bounced off and they gave Augie an error on that.

The first ball that was hit to me at third base down there, I dove toward third base and knocked the ball down and they gave me an error. I think at that time what they was tryin' to do, they was tryin' to psyche me out, but they were wrong. They were dead wrong.

The old boys got the breaks and they still do. I was a young guy and they wasn't gonna make it easy for me. That's to be expected. I didn't let that bother me; I had a job to do and I did it.

BK: Your hustle at that time turned the Series in Detroit's favor.

FC: Mickey knew that. He knew that I would be playin' second base for about four or five teams in that league, but they wasn't about to sell me at that time. I understood this, but that was my ambition—to play ball with Detroit and I was gonna make the best of it.

Flea Clifton (courtesy National Pastime).

BK: You played in Detroit through '37 and then spent several years in the minors.

FC: I played two years at Toronto. I played 16 all together. I played a little bit over at Syracuse and I played at Minneapolis, had a real good year. I could've gone back to the big leagues from there, and then I played a year down in Fort Worth with Rogers Hornsby.

I enjoyed playing for Rog. He was a smart manager. I learned a lot from him, but I learned it 10 years too late—about hitting. Ol' Rog was somethin' else, I'll tell you. I never had a bit of trouble. I enjoyed playin' for him. I used to see him sit around—he'd check on some of these guys, check the lobby at night. One time, I says, "Rog, you never say a word to me." He said, "Hell, I don't need to. You wanta play baseball." That's all he said.

The other story he told me I never forgot. Judge Landis told him, said, "Roger, you give up playin' the horses and there's four or five big league jobs waitin' for you." I said, "Rog, what did you say to him?" He said, "Well, very simple: 'Judge, if you give up playin' the stock market, I'll give up playin' the horses.'" (Laughs)

I went into insurance when I quit playin'. The only reason I took that job was because I could control my time to the point where I could fool around with kids. I had a lot of Knothole teams around Cincinnati where I could spend my time with these kids and teach 'em how to play the game. Of course, I always taught 'em three things: the first thing I taught 'em was manners, the second thing I taught 'em was how to take care of themselves, and then the third and last thing I taught 'em was how to play baseball.

BK: Was there one game that stands out?

FC: The one game that always sticks in my mind, and there's only one guy I was thinkin' of, it was the second year and we were playin' Washington. It was a tight ballgame. Jo Jo White was hittin' and I was on second base. I heard Buddy [Myer] say to the shortstop, "We have a fast man. Go for the double [play] but we gotta make sure we get the one man." I can't think of the shortstop's name offhand.

I don't know, but I was probably near third base and roundin' the bag and Baker was givin' me the stop sign. I didn't pay no mind, I just kept goin'—and ol' Ty was ridin' right with me. They tell me [Pete] Susko, the first baseman, jumped about a foot or two foot up in the air and I beat the play easy to home plate. So that was the one and I thought of Ty Cobb at the time.

Mickey, when I came in, said to me, "Hey, Flea, you know what?" I said, "No. What?" He says, "Nice goin', but if you didn't make it it would've taken $25 to buy a postal card to send back to let me know where you were." (Laughs) I said, "Mike, there was no doubt in my mind I was gonna make it. Ty Cobb made it, now I made it."

Del Baker was the coach and he said he had me goin' all the way. (Laughs) He had both hands up in the air, stoppin' me. We beat Washington, 2 to 1. Tommy Bridges was pitchin'.

Tommy had that great curve and he couldn't show anybody else how to throw it. It was terrific to see the break he could get on that ball and he would take pitchers and show 'em how he held that ball and how he could make it break, but no one was ever able to throw that curveball like he could. It was tremendous.

In the World Series he struck out that Jurges up there. Three or four curveballs he threw Jurges started shoulder high and Mickey was catchin' 'em at the ankles!

We had a sayin' for a good curveball: "It would drop off the table." I have never heard of or seen a curveball like Tommy Bridges's. And he wasn't a big man—he wasn't as big as I was.

There was one team that wore him out. That was Washington. Somehow or other, that Washington ballclub, when Tommy would throw his super-duper curveball or fastball—no matter what he threw—they wore Tommy out. Washington had a real good ballclub, a good hittin' ballclub.

Walter Johnson was retired, but he was with the ballclub. I was always one of the first—I'd get out on the bench to see what these other hitters looked like. Walter was out there—I didn't know him, he looked like a big plow jockey. Mickey and Cy Perkins came out and I said to Mike, "Mike, who is that big plow jockey out there?" He says, "Why?" I said, "They're havin' a hell of a time hittin' this guy in battin' practice." He and Cy Perkins liked to have busted a gut at that. (Laughs) He says, "That's Walter Johnson!"

He was out there, just whippin' that ball in there. That Washington had a good hittin' ballclub and they were hittin' him.

BK: Who was the best player you saw?

FC: That's pretty hard to pick that one out. Mickey, undoubtedly, was my pet, but on the opposition you'd have to take Lefty Grove, somebody like that.

Course, Babe Ruth and the Yankees, they had an old ballclub. They were on the tail end of their careers at that time—Ruth and Gehrig. They had Dickey catchin'. They had a good ballclub, a real good ballclub, but the Babe was havin' leg trouble like Lazzeri and as the year went on we caught 'em and went ahead and beat 'em. They had Combs in center field and then DiMaggio came along. He was a hell of a ballplayer.

BK: Did you save souvenirs along the way?

FC: I wouldn't have had a thing if it hadn't been for my wife. She kept it. Newspapers never bothered me, I never saved 'em.

The old boys that I knew—fans and what have you—they're gone. I had a chance to do one of these card shows up at Detroit and I turned it down. Billy Rogell was gonna be up there and I would've loved to be up there with him. All expenses paid and $750 or so. I told Billy, I said, "I couldn't take money—10, 15, 20 dollars—to sign something for some kid when I would do it for nothin'."

That was Babe Ruth's thinkin'. My whole life I never charged for anything. In a year's time, I get 200, 300 requests. They come in—balls, bats, anything they have. Whatever they send, I sign it and send it back.

BK: What about today's game compared to the game in your day?

FC: I always have a stock answer for that. The paying customers are the ones who make the product. If they like the product, they come out to see it. They're the ones who make that decision.

I'd like to make the bucks they're makin' today, but the owners in the time that I played didn't have the TV money that these boys today have to throw around.

I don't watch it on TV and I don't listen to it. I'm active with the kids. After I quit I did a little scoutin' for the Reds but the only district I would do would be the local district around town here. I had no desire to stay in the game. I guess I could've stayed in in some capacity. I guess I didn't care too much about that travellin' and stayin' away from home. I had three kids, so when I quit, I quit and walked away.

BK: Any regrets?

FC: None whatsoever.

BK: Would you do it again?

FC: Sure, if I could make it where I could go play at Detroit. I wanted to play where and *as* Ty Cobb played the game. I patterned my whole life after Ty—his health habits and his way and his sense of honor about things in general. Like I said, he was my patron saint.

Herman Earl (Flea) Clifton

Born December 12, 1909, Cincinnati, OH
Ht. 5′10″ Wt. 160 Batted and Threw Right

Year	Team	G	AB	R	H	2B	3B	HR	RBI	SB	BA	SA
1934	DetA	16	16	3	1	0	0	0	1	0	.063	.063
1935		43	110	15	28	5	0	0	9	2	.255	.300
1936		13	26	5	5	1	0	0	1	0	.192	.231
1937		15	43	4	5	1	0	0	2	3	.116	.140
4 years		87	195	27	39	7	0	0	13	5	.200	.236

World Series

Year	Team	G	AB	R	H	2B	3B	HR	RBI	SB	BA	SA
1935	DetA	4	16	1	0	0	0	0	0	0	.000	.000

JACK WILSON

Red Sox Ace

1934–1942

The Boston Red Sox of the late 1930s were not unlike the Boston Red Sox of most any time: good hitting, questionable pitching. The likes of Jimmie Foxx, Doc Cramer, Bobby Doerr, Ted Williams, Ben Chapman, Pinky Higgins, and Joe Cronin were on the team from 1937 through 1940, and the Red Sox had the highest cumulative batting average in the major leagues.

But the pitching staff was as it always seems to be: two or three good

Above: **Jack Wilson (George Brace photo).**

hurlers and a bunch of other guys who could throw the ball 60 feet, more or less. Perhaps the oddest part of this tale is that the pitching staff was relatively stable during this period—the same guys were there every year. It would certainly seem that a little of the offense could have been traded for some pitching, but it was not.

The frontline pitchers were good, however; there just were not enough of them. Anchoring the staff for these four seasons were a righty and a lefty. The southpaw was the immortal Lefty Grove; the right hander was Jack Wilson.

Wilson appeared in more games in that period than any other Red Sox hurler, and he divided them fairly evenly between starting and relieving—86 starts and 70 trips from the bullpen. Not many fans know that from 1937 through 1940 Jack Wilson won more games than Grove—or any other Red Sox pitcher for that matter. He won 54 games in those four seasons. Grove won 53. No one else on the team won over 31.

Wilson left the majors after 1942. In 1994 he was elected to the Oregon Hall of Fame.

* * *

BK: You were a third baseman originally. When did you become a pitcher?

JACK WILSON: In 1932, I started out as a third baseman and I just got to where I made more errors throwing than anything, so somebody decided I should be a pitcher.

I belonged to the San Francisco Seals at the time and they wanted me to go back down to Arizona again. I had a pretty good year down there and I didn't want to go back because I was afraid the league would blow up and it did.

So I went home to Portland and I was playing semipro ball around there, and I decided one day that I'd like to give that pitching a try. That's how I started and before the '32 summer was over I signed with Portland of the Pacific Coast League.

I was nothing great the next few years, but by '34 I was going pretty good and I went to the Athletics. Connie Mack sent me back to Portland. Earl Sheely was just made a scout for the Red Sox and [Joe] Cronin had just gone over there as manager and I was the first ballplayer they bought. That's how I got to the big leagues.

BK: Your first hit for Boston was a game-winning home run in the eleventh inning against Washington.

JW: I went in to relieve Wes Ferrell in the second inning. We were being beat, 9 to 2, I think it was. I went in and hung on there till the eleventh inning. Cronin hit a home run in the eighth inning with the bases loaded and we tied, and I hit one in the center field bleachers there in Boston and we won. Billy Rogell with Detroit and Jimmie Foxx with Philadelphia had hit 'em there, but I was the first one from the Red Sox to do it. It was a pretty fair cast at that time.

That was my biggest thrill in baseball and I remember that *real* well. (Laughs) I don't remember going around the bases, but I remember hitting it.

BK: Who was the pitcher?

JW: A fellow named Phil Hensiek, and he was in Chattanooga the next day. (Laughs)

Old Eddie Collins—he was the general manager—he gave me hell the next day for swinging at a bad pitch. It was funny, really. I went down in the clubhouse and told a couple of guys there, "That damn Collins is giving me hell about swinging at a bad pitch." They said, "Hell, don't pay attention to him."

We had a lot of guys from the Athletics over there: Grove and [Rube] Walberg and [Max] Bishop, then Foxx came later. About took the whole club, really. He [Mack] was getting rid of 'em. He just got through getting rid of [Jimmy] Dykes and [Al] Simmons and [Mule] Haas to Chicago. Later on, Foxx and [Johnny] Marcum and [Doc] Cramer and Dib Williams and a whole bunch of 'em came to Boston.

BK: You had a lot of hitting there in Boston, but the pitching was thin.

JW: We didn't do much and we couldn't beat the Yankees. They talk about the '27 team, but they had [Lefty] Gomez and [Red] Ruffing and [Spud] Chandler and Monte Pearson and Bump Hadley and that bunch, and they had, God knows, a better catcher in Bill Dickey.

I've said this before. I don't know if Mickey Mantle would have made that club for one reason: [Charlie] Keller and [Joe] DiMaggio and [Tommy] Henrich were a great outfield and I don't know where he'd have played. The infield was [Lou] Gehrig and [Tony] Lazzeri and [Frank] Crosetti and Red Rolfe. They were pretty tough. You get the first two out or else you're in trouble.

BK: For many years, you started and relieved interchangeably. Did you have a preference?

JW: I liked to start, but I'd start and go nine innings. But Cronin ruined my career. I hurt my arm pitching today and tomorrow and the next day and then starting. It was nothing to pitch nine innings today and go down in the bullpen and go in and save one the next day, but they didn't count saves in those days.

[Saves have now been calculated for years before they were an official statistic. Wilson was third in the American League in 1937 and fourth in 1940. He was second in games twice, 1937 and 1940, and third in 1936. In 1937, he pitched in 51 games, 21 of them starts. The league leader that season was Clint Brown of Chicago; he pitched in 53 games with no starts.]

BK: Elden Auker said the worst year he ever had was the year he played under Cronin. He was not thrilled with him as a handler of pitchers.

JW: You better believe it. Nobody else was. He ruined more good young pitchers than anybody. [Bill] Butland and [Woody] Rich and Mickey Harris—he didn't help them, either.

Joe was a funny guy. He thought that nobody could have a sore arm because Walter Johnson never had a sore arm. Nobody could ever be hurt because Walter Johnson was never hurt. He hit a home run in Philadelphia and he was watching it go in the upper deck and turned his ankle on first base. When he come in, I said, "Now go out there and fight 'em, Joe! Damn it, you're not hurt! Nobody can be hurt!" He went out there but he walked in after about ten minutes. It was hurt bad.

He was a hunch player and everything else. He got us in a lot of trouble. We had Grove and [Bobo] Newsom and myself to pitch a three-game series against the Yankees and we were all gone after the first game. They got Grove out there and he put Newsom in and then he put me in to finish it and I lost it in about the fifteenth inning. He didn't have anybody to pitch the next two games with any rest. (Laughs)

He'd do some other crazy things. He'd send guys ahead to New York to pitch and then he wouldn't pitch 'em the first day over there. He'd wait a day or two. He did that with Rube Walberg and myself. We were sent over there and the next day we had a doubleheader in Yankee Stadium and he pitched somebody else.

He lasted a long time as a manager because he sat on Yawkey's lap. That's enough on him. You get the idea, I think.

BK: You had another big day with the bat in 1940.

JW: That was in Chicago. I remember that real well. (Laughs)

I've got three grandsons that are all baseball nuts. One of 'em's out of college, one's getting out, and the other one's got a couple of years. He's on a baseball scholarship at Walla Walla Community College now. I tell 'em about that hitting.

I hit one off Jack Knott. I hit that in the upper deck at Comiskey Park. The other one was off Pete Appleton. His original name was Jablonowski. He pitched for Cleveland and Washington before he went over to Chicago.

The funny thing, Sheely was there that day. He had just come in from the West Coast. They used to bring scouts in then to take a look at who they

Jack Wilson (courtesy National Pastime).

were scouting, so they'd have an idea of what they were looking for. I was supposed to have dinner with him that night—we were real close friends—and I couldn't find him. I found afterwards he told a couple of 'em, "Hell, I wasn't about to sit there and eat dinner and listen to him talk about his hitting." (Laughs)

BK: Those were the only three home runs you hit, but you were a good hitting pitcher.

JW: I hit pretty good. One of my grandsons looked it up and said I hit

.199 for my career. I said, "By God, that's more than some are hitting now, anyway." [Wilson batted .313 in 1935 and .273 in 1940.]

BK: You only dropped below .200 in your last season when you went 2 for 18 with Washington and Detroit.

JW: That was a sad year when I was traded to Washington. That Cronin—I saw him in San Francisco after the '41 season. I played golf with him and Ty Cobb and Tony Lazzeri. I went down to see him on purpose 'cause I knew the newspapers were on me pretty bad. My arm wasn't so good and I knew they were *trying* to trade me.

I asked him, "Do me a favor; don't trade me to St. Louis or Washington."

A newspaperman named Holly Goodrich called me up one night in Portland in the wintertime and says, "Well, what do you think of it?"

"Think of what?"

"Don't you know?"

"Know what?"

"You've been traded to Washington."

I couldn't believe it. I hung up the phone and I actually cried.

I didn't have much of a year of '42 at all.

BK: You were only in Washington about half the year.

JW: They took Social Security out up to a certain point and then you were through for the year. When I went to Detroit they took it out before I knew it and I got the same amount there, so it was exactly a half a year.

BK: Was it better in Detroit than in Washington?

JW: Oh, yeah. A lot better. Of course, [Hank] Greenberg was gone and they didn't have too much going for 'em right about that time in '41.

BK: Did you go in the service after that?

JW: No. I stayed home. I could have gone to Cleveland when Del Baker was over there, but I didn't go back because of the draft deal and there was no sense in going back, I figured.

I registered in Somerville, Massachusetts, when I had to register. There were no airplanes in those days and I'd get the mail on Friday or something telling me to report on Monday morning. I'd write 'em and I'd be reclassified another time.

I finally went up and they found out that I'd had arthritis or something in my elbow. There were chipped bones in there that I'd had checked out once before and he [the doctor] never would tell me the results of the x-rays. I never knew what it was till I went to the doctor in Portland.

Dr. Kimberley operated on my arm and he sent a letter in and told 'em I had arthritis and what the operation had been and the guys says, "Then nobody'll be calling you. Do whatever you want."

So I didn't go in the service at all. I played at Portland after that. They made a deal with Jack Zeller [Detroit general manager] to get me out here so I could pitch.

That was '44 and there wasn't much doing. I beat around, and then I managed for a couple of years at Salem in the Western International League. Before that I coached a year at Portland University.

BK: Would you go back and play baseball again?

JW: If I had it to do over I would, but I'd have one stipulation—there'd be nobody named Cronin around.

BK: Any regrets?

JW: No. I really don't. I'd like to have some of the money these guys are getting now.

BK: A pitcher who wins 12 to 16 games a year today is getting two or three million.

JW: (Laughs) I would think. When I went to Washington, old man Griffith cut me $4,000. That was a lot of money then.

We went back to Boston and Bucky Harris [Senators' manager] asked, "Do you want to pitch the opener over there?" And I said, "Hell, yes!" So I went over and beat 'em, 10 to 3, and I would have beat 'em, 10 to nothing, but a guy hit a swinging bunt down third base. The third baseman's name was [Bobby] Estalella and he was Cuban supposedly, but he was pretty black. He threw it as far as he could in that right-field corner and that's how they got the three runs. (Laughs)

Going up the runway, somebody put his arm around me and says, "How they going?" I turned around and looked at him and it was Cronin. I says, "Everything's fine but that son-of-a-bitching father-in-law of yours."

And that was the end of everything. Ed Daugherty was in public relations, then he went in the service and then they gave him a ball club—Scranton—to run and he asked me if I'd manage it and I said yeah. He called me and told me I had the job, and then he wrote me a letter and told me that Cronin, who was then the general manager of the Red Sox, said that I wasn't going to manage the ball club and that was it.

Bobby Doerr was scouting for the Red Sox and he asked me over in Spokane one day, "What in the hell ever happened? All these donkeys get jobs around someplace. All you did for him, why didn't he give you a job?"

I told him. He said, "That's the reason!" (Laughs)

BK: Who was the best hitter or best player you saw?

JW: I didn't run around with him personally, even when I could have when he'd come to see Dom, but Joe [DiMaggio] was the best ballplayer. The best hitter—there'll never be another one—was Ted Williams. He was just uncanny.

Big John Rigney, pitching for the White Sox, come up to the top one time Ted popped the pitch up. He said, "You know, he did something up at the top there and took a little off it. I'll nail the ball and hit it out of the park next time up." And he did. He come back and said, "He did it again." I never saw what he did but Ted must've. He knew what he was talking about.

I wish Foxx had been in this world to hit that ball they're hitting now. Foxx hit balls over the top of that Comiskey Park like they were going out of style. There are places he hit 'em and you wouldn't believe it.

Johnny Pesky was a hell of a ballplayer. I took him to spring training gave him gloves and sweatshirts and everything. He was over in Bradenton and we were in Sarasota and he told me he wanted to come home, he was homesick. [Herb] Pennock was talking to him and we had him around there at Sarasota for about three days. My wife would cook for him and he got over being homesick.

Heinie Manush wound up being his manager there at Rocky Mount. He's the one John gives most of the credit for his hitting—he got 200 hits his first year. He was the most valuable player in that league [Piedmont].

The next year he was picked as the most outstanding player at Louisville in the American Association. We owned [Pee Wee] Reese but Cronin wouldn't bring him up. He [Cronin] was the worst shortstop that God ever created. He might have been a wonder over there at Washington when he was young, but not when I saw him. Finally they brought John up and, by God, I get traded. (Laughs) It made me sick.

BK: Did you get to see Babe Ruth play?

JW: Thirty-four was his last year in the AL. I was over at Philadelphia—that's when I first went up—and we went over [to New York] but he didn't play. One thing for damned sure, he was the greatest as far as I'm concerned—as a hitter, you know, and what he did for baseball. He saved the game.

BK: You didn't face Williams often. Who was the toughest hitter on you?

JW: I got to pitch to him in that game in Boston. I threw him a knuckleball just for meanness and he hit a screaming line drive to right field and Bruce Campbell—he'd come over to Washington from Detroit—caught it. He said, "I don't know what in the hell you threw him, but don't throw it anymore!" (Laughs)

The guy that hit me better than anybody was a guy named Rip Radcliff for the White Sox. He'd tell me the last time we'd see him [each season], "Now be real careful this winter and don't let anything happen to you so you're sure to be back." (Laughs)

He hit Feller good, too. He'd hit line drives all day long. He was a good ballplayer.

BK: Who was the best pitcher you saw?

JW: The best pitcher I ever saw was Satchel Paige. I saw him in 1933 down in Los Angeles at night. We had an all-star club supposedly out of the Coast League and we had some good ballplayers—guys that had been around.

He only pitched three innings and he struck out the first two and then Earl Sheely fouled out to the catcher. Then he struck out the next six. Sheely was kidding about it afterwards. He said, "I must be a hell of a hitter. I at least fouled one." (Laughs) Paige could do anything with a ball.

The kid I used to always pitch against—Feller—he was a hell of a pitcher, too. They'd skip my turn in St. Louis and every place else so I could pitch against him and I beat him more than he did me.

BK: I understand that Grove, since he was allowed to pick his starts, chose to skip Feller.

JW: He was a funny guy. Very bad disposition. He went for a month there and wouldn't talk to anybody on the ball club. Foxx dropped a pop fly, would've been the third out in Chicago, and somebody got a base hit and they scored. We went to the twelfth inning and won against Ted Lyons.

The next morning, when old Tom Yawkey come down walking through the lobby, he said, "Good morning, Mose." He said, "What the fuck's good about it!" And he never talked to us. He went for a month and when he wanted to talk to us we got tongue-tied.

He had a very bad disposition. He was different from anybody that I ever knew, really. He could be as nice a guy as you'd ever want to see.

He was a banker on the road. He enjoyed doing that. He'd go around with seven, eight hundred dollars in his pocket. We wouldn't have to write checks and every payday when we'd get home, he'd say "Everybody that owes, pay me."

We had some good pitchers. Wes Ferrell was there. Of course, Wes had lost his fastball by that time. But in the spring, it was Grove and Ferrell and then rain. That's like that Spahn and Sain deal. At times, the two of 'em did all the pitching. It rained in Boston, I can tell you that.

I saw Joe Morgan [former Red Sox manager] when they were out here. Never met him [before]. He made the remark to somebody and they told me about it. He said I was the best cool weather pitcher he'd ever seen, so I *had* to talk to him. (Laughs) I went out to the ballpark and whether he wins or not or whether he's a great manager, he's a hell of a good guy to talk to.

BK: Do you get much fan mail today?

JW: I'll probably get about five or six letters a month.

There are these guys around that are charging [for autographs]. Like I said, I never was a great friend of DiMaggio even though I knew his brother and Dominic played with us. I was amazed to hear that he went to these places and charged for his autograph. All the money that he's got. I can't understand that! Damned if I can! It just doesn't seem right. I'd feel pretty bad about charging.

There's a book out that has the addresses. Every once in a while I'll think of somebody and take a look to see if they're alive or dead. (Laughs) There's not many left.

There's a guy I talked to about putting a new roof on the house. He gave me two prices and said one was because it had a 20-year guarantee. I said, "I'm over 80 years old! I'm worried about a 20-year guarantee?!" (Laughs)

John Francis (Black Jack) Wilson

Born April 12, 1912, Portland, OR
Ht. 5′11″ Wt. 210 Batted and Threw Right

Year	Team	G	IP	W	L	PCT	BB	SO	H	SHO	SV	ERA
1934	PhiA	2	9	0	1	.000	9	2	15	0	0	12.00
1935	BosA	23	64	3	4	.429	36	19	72	0	1	4.22
1936		43	136.1	6	8	.429	86	74	152	0	3	4.42
1937		51	221.1	16	10	.615	119	137	209	1	7	3.70
1938		37	194.2	15	15	.500	91	96	200	3	1	4.30
1939		36	177.1	11	11	.500	75	60	198	0	2	4.67
1940		41	157.2	12	6	.667	87	102	170	0	5	5.08
1941		27	116.1	4	12	.235	70	55	140	1	1	5.03
1942	WasA	12	42	1	4	.200	23	18	57	0	0	6.64
	DetA	9	13	0	0	.000	5	7	10	0	0	4.85
9 years		281	1131.2	68	72	.486	601	590	1233	5	20	4.59

HARRY EISENSTAT

Under Control

1935–1942

On October 2, 1938, Bob Feller set a new record for strikeouts in a game. He fanned 18 Detroit Tigers that day. Birdie Tebbetts caught for

Above: **Harry Eisenstat (George Brace photo).**

Detroit in that game. Tebbetts said, as quoted by Ira Berkow in *Hank Greenberg: The Story of My Life*, "Feller was throwing the ball at about 105 miles an hour. . . . He just mowed us down. [Detroit pitcher Harry] Eisenstat was throwing the ball at about 81 miles an hour and struck out three guys. And he beat Feller."

Harry Eisenstat, a Brooklyn-born lefty, tossed a four-hitter that day and defeated Feller and the Indians, 4 to 1.

Eisenstat was a reliever and spot starter for the Tigers that season. He had signed as a free agent before the season at the encouragement of his friend and fellow New Yorker, Hank Greenberg.

This was the season—1938—that Greenberg hammered 58 home runs and Eisenstat proved helpful to his friend. When big Hank would get into a slump, Harry would pitch extra batting practice for him, emulating the pitcher Greenberg was to face in the next game.

Harry's time in Detroit was short, though—a little over one season. He was traded to Cleveland for Earl Averill and toiled for the Tribe until he joined the Air Force in 1943. Although only 30 when he came back out in '46, he left the game to enter the business world. Today, nearing eighty, he is still active.

* * *

BK: You're from Brooklyn and you played with the Dodgers as a teenager.

HARRY EISENSTAT: I was signed by the Brooklyn Dodgers by Casey Stengel. Al Lopez was the catcher at that time.

Then they sent me to Dayton, which was one of their farm teams. Dayton, Ohio. I pitched for the Dayton Ducks and I won 18 and lost 6 and we won the pennant in 1935. And then in 1936 I was sent to Allentown, which was Class A, and I won 21 and lost 8.

The next year I went to spring training with the Dodgers and I was sent to Louisville in Double-A ball. I was with Brooklyn for about a month or so and then I went to Louisville. I won about 12 at that time in a little over a half of the year—12 and 5, 12 and 6—I forget exactly. In between those times I stayed with Brooklyn and pitched a little with the Dodgers.

At that time, I was declared a free agent by Judge Landis. They had some rule at that time that you could farm a ballplayer out three times. In 1934 I pitched for the Dodgers for about a month when I got out of school. The next year they sent me to Dayton. Well, they felt that was considered a year and Judge Landis declared me a free agent. Then I signed with the

Detroit Tigers because I was quite friendly with Hank Greenberg. He was from New York as well and we were quite close. He said they needed left-handed pitching and I would do well with them.

BK: In '38 you were the number one man out of the bullpen for the Tigers.

HE: Right. I think I won 9 and lost 6 in 1938. That was the year that Bob Feller struck out 18 men, established a world's strikeout record, and I beat him that day, 4 to 1.

I was with Detroit in '38 and in '39 I was traded during the season. I won a doubleheader against Philadelphia. I won both games of a doubleheader—pitched five innings in one game and four innings in another game and got credit for both games and Hank Greenberg hit three home runs. [Eisenstat did not allow any runs on the day.]

Then I was traded to Cleveland for Earl Averill and I left Detroit and relieved most of the time.

BK: Were you happy as a reliever?

HE: Yes, as long as I pitched I had no objections.

BK: You had some good games as a starter and completed a good percent of your starts.

HE: I wasn't a steady starter, but I filled in when doubleheaders piled up.

I went to Cleveland in '39 and then I went into service [in 1943]. I went into the Air Force, and when I got out of service I decided I wanted to go into business here. I had been in the hardware business while I was with Detroit. I had worked for a company and I liked it very much.

When I got out of service, I was still the property of Cleveland and I decided at that time I wanted to raise a family and it was kind of difficult as a ballplayer. I decided to stay in Cleveland and I went into the hardware business.

I was in the hardware business for 20 years here in Cleveland—in Shaker Heights—and then after the hardware business—I sold out—I've been vice president in the national accounts for Curtis Industries. I still work one or two days a week. They wanted me to stay on to take care of some of the accounts we had opened up over the years.

BK: You worked in a defense plant for a while during the war.

HE: Yes, just for a short period of time. That was just in the wintertime, then I went into service.

BK: The Indians were just short of being a really good team when you were there.

HE: We had good pitching at that time. We lost out in 1940. Detroit beat us out of the pennant at the end of the season. Floyd Giebell pitched

Harry Eisenstat (courtesy National Pastime).

and beat Feller, 2 to nothing I believe, and they won the pennant on that.

BK: You were a heck of a good hitting pitcher.

HE: Well, I lucked out and got a couple of hits but I wouldn't consider myself an outstanding hitter. [He was; his career average was a solid .211.]

BK: For a lefthander, you had great control.

HE: Yeah, that's one thing. I could throw the ball pretty much where I liked. I could throw the ball well. I had excellent control. Mickey Cochrane was our manager in Detroit and he used me and he always felt that I had outstanding control.

BK: Is there one game that stands out in your memory?

HE: The game that stands out is when Bob Feller struck out 18 men and established the world's record. That was the year Greenberg had 58 home runs and threatened Babe Ruth's record.

BK: Did they pitch to him at the end?

HE: Yes, they did. He hit some balls. He got a couple of hits. He faced Feller at the end, but he wasn't able to break the record. He was a great hitter. He made himself a great ballplayer. He worked at it. Today a lot of the ballplayers don't work at it. They come to the ballpark with attaché cases and their agents.

BK: Who was the best hitter or best player you saw?

HE: One of the greatest, I thought, was Charlie Gehringer. He was a great, great second baseman and he's a Hall of Famer.

And I would say Joe DiMaggio, as far as a hitter. And Ted Williams.

BK: What about the best pitcher?

HE: I would choose Bob Feller as the best. I would choose Red Ruffing as a great pitcher. Tommy Bridges, Schoolboy Rowe.

BK: Mel Harder?

HE: Mel Harder was a *great* pitcher. Great curveball. He's a good friend of mine and I'm rather disappointed that he didn't get into the Hall of Fame. And he's a gentleman—a class guy.

BK: How much fan mail do you receive?

HE: Oh, I get three, four a week. Cards, pictures, and they send envelopes. I'm always glad to sign, but what has happened today is a lot of guys are using ballplayers. I get mail many times from the same people—two, three, four times. They are abusive; they're exploiting it and they're selling them. I'm not saying mine is worth so much or anything like that—it really isn't. I just don't like to get involved. I'm glad to cooperate, but I don't like to get the same ones I've gotten in the past.

I have no objections to baseball fans or to collectors that have their own collections for their youngsters. That part I have no objection to, but I object to the same guys—I recognize the name immediately and what city it's from and so on.

BK: Any regrets?

HE: No, I didn't have any regrets. I enjoyed it; it was great while I played.

The only regret I probably have is that I didn't stay to get my college degree. If I were to go back, that's the only thing I would do differently. I went a couple of years and that was it. You make decisions at that time if you mature a little bit you wouldn't have made.

BK: Would you be a ballplayer again?

HE: Yes.

Harry Eisenstat

Born October 10, 1915, Brooklyn, NY
Ht. 5'11" Wt. 185 Batted and Threw Left

Year	Team	G	IP	W	L	PCT	BB	SO	H	SHO	SV	ERA
1935	BrkN	2	4.2	0	1	.000	2	2	9	0	0	13.50
1936		5	14.1	1	2	.333	6	5	22	0	0	5.65
1937		13	47.2	3	3	.500	11	12	61	0	0	3.97
1938	DetA	32	125.1	9	6	.600	29	37	131	0	4	3.73
1939	DetA	10	29.2	2	2	.500	9	6	39	0	0	6.98
	CleA	26	103.2	6	7	.462	23	38	109	1	2	3.30
1940	CleA	27	71.2	1	4	.200	12	27	78	0	4	3.14
1941		21	34	1	1	.500	16	11	43	0	2	4.24
1942		29	47.2	2	1	.667	6	19	58	0	2	2.45
8 years		165	478.2	25	27	.481	114	157	550	1	14	3.84

BUDDY HASSETT

A Vanishing Breed

1936–1942

Buddy Hassett did not strike out very often. At one time, batters who did not strike out often were not unusual. For instance, in 1936, Buddy's rookie year, there were 24 regular major league players (players with at least 400 at-bats) who fanned fewer than 25 times. Only Jimmy Foxx whiffed over 100 times.

***Above:* Buddy Hassett (George Brace photo).**

Fifty years later Bill Buckner was the only regular major league player (there were about 190) who had 25 Ks and he had exactly 25. Thirty-four men topped the 100 strikeout mark.

Over the years, several men have averaged over 30 at-bats per strikeout, but the last year any of them played was 1965 (Nellie Fox), and before that it was 1952 (Tommy Holmes). Thus, only two batters in the last 50 years had a good enough eye and good enough bat control to fan only once every seven or eight games. Before that, though, there were several and Buddy Hassett was one of the best.

Because of the presence of Lou Gehrig and the advent of World War II, Buddy spent only seven years in the big leagues. Originally signed by the Yankees in the early 1930s, the first baseman spent several years in the minors. After all, no one was going to beat out Gehrig.

He requested that the team deal him so he could get a shot at the major leagues and the Yankees complied. He joined the Brooklyn Dodgers in 1936 and became their first baseman.

He had a fantastic rookie year. He laid claim to first base and played every game (a league-leading 156), batted .310, drove in 82 runs and scored 79, both team-leading totals, and, in 635 at bats, struck out only 17 times. Let's repeat that: 17 Ks in 635 ABs. And as a rookie, no less.

The sophomore jinx was no problem. His average "dipped" to .304 and his strikeouts shot up to 19, the most he would ever have in a major league season.

He stayed in the big league through 1942, when he finally became the Yankees' first sacker. Then World War II abruptly ended his career. In his seven seasons, Hassett had 3,517 at bats in 929 games and fanned only 116 times, or once every 30 at-bats.

Hassett holds one National League record—he had ten consecutive hits. Since 1900, six National Leaguers have done that, but no one has ever topped it.

Hassett was a marvelous hitter with marvelous bat control. He is almost forgotten today, but the next time you see a .240 hitter strike out three times in a game, remember that there was once a .300 hitter who did not strike out three times a month.

*   *   *

BK: I'm sure a lot of baseball fans never heard of you.

BUDDY HASSETT: I know that. (Laughs)

BK: Your strike-out record is one of the best of all time.

BH: As I wrote you, I'm surprised that someone picked up on that.

BK: You evidently had fantastic bat control; the most you ever struck out in a major league season was 19 times.

BH: That's right. I never made 20.

BK: How did you have such great bat control?

BH: When I was in college I could hit the long ball pretty well and then I got into professional baseball in Wheeling and we played six days at night. Only on Sunday did you see the daylight. You have that today, the same thing.

I decided if I was going to advance myself I better have a batting average more than a home run average. At that time, if you didn't hit around .300 in the minors you didn't move. They didn't care how many home runs you hit—they weren't looking at that that much. They were looking at your batting average and whether you were able to play every day. Those were the two things that would determine whether you'd move along in an organization such as the Yankees, which I was brought up in before I was sold to Brooklyn.

I decided then to try to meet the ball and I guess I cut down on the bat a little bit—I had a little bit of the bat hanging out the bottom of my hands—so I had better control of the barrel of the bat. It's a matter of eyes and muscle control, but I always tried to get a piece of the ball.

If you notice, I didn't get too many bases on balls, either. I believed if you were gonna play, the idea was to hit the ball.

BK: How many of your strikeouts would you say were swinging?

BH: I'd say very few. Most of 'em were calls. When it was a borderline [pitch] I was swinging. I'd try to get a piece of the ball, whether it be one way or the other.

But as I got along in major league baseball, I tended to hit the ball more to the opposite field, and it wasn't until I got talking to Frank Frisch one day and he said, "Bud, you got to learn to pull the ball." He was then doing the broadcasting with the Braves when I was playing for [Casey] Stengel, around 1941. I decided to try to learn to pull the ball again. I had done it when I was younger, but when I got into night baseball I decided to make sure I got a piece of the ball.

When I went to the Yankees it was a pleasure because I finally got to where I could pull the ball, and then I could go either way—I could go to left field or right field.

I could run pretty good, so I could get some bunts in there, too, and I guess I legged out a few here and there.

BK: Where did you go to college?

BH: Manhattan College in New York. Played baseball and basketball.

I signed with the Yankees when I got through college in 1933 and they sent me to Wheeling that year. I hit about .332 there, then they sent me to Norfolk, where I had a very good year. I hit about .360 and broke the league record for stolen bases with 56. It held up for 20 years in the Piedmont League.

BK: In the time you were in the major leagues, bases were not being stolen.

BH: You weren't allowed to. You were told when to go.

I look at this player who was over there with the Mets and I just laugh. They said they give him the green light and to me he's broken up more rallies for them. (Laughs) He gets thrown out and he says, "I'm told to steal bases," but when I played the manager told you when to steal. That's what he got paid for. They've got to think before they run.

(Laughs) Talking about thinking, I remember something that happened to me my first year at Wheeling. Jack Sheehan, who later became in charge of the minor leagues for the Cubs in about 1948 or '49 when I was managing Newark for the Yankees, was the manager. I was playing for him and we were about three or four runs behind and I was on first base. I thought I saw the steal sign and I took off and I was thrown out from here to the wall. Jack was a playing manager, but he was still coaching at third base and our dugout was at third base, so when I'm thrown out at second I have to come by him.

I walked by and Jack said, "Hey, Bud. What happened?" I said, "Gee, Mr. Sheehan, I thought . . ."

He said, "Stop right there. Don't go to thinking; you'll weaken the ball club." (Laughs)

I learned a lesson right there—I better watch for the signs. But I see so many signs missed here in this baseball that people just gloss over. When I played, you'd be fined.

Getting back to the strikeouts, it was the control of the bat. As I said, I didn't hit too many home runs because of that. My job, I figured, was to get on base if I could and that's all I tried to do.

BK: Where did you usually bat in the order?

BH: With Brooklyn I was third, fourth. The first year, because we didn't do too well, I was all over. I think I drove in 80-some-odd runs. They generally kept me from fifth on down and then sometimes leadoff.

BK: In 1940, you equalled the National League record for consecutive hits.

BH: When you're doing it, you don't think about it. You just keep going and going as far as you can go. When it's over, then somebody tells you. I didn't give it a thought while I was doing it.

Buddy Hassett (courtesy National Pastime).

BK: You asked the Yankees to get you to another team.

BH: Naturally. With Lou Gehrig playing there, what else would you want? (Laughs)

I had nice friends. The fellow who signed me, Paul Krichell, was one of the finest men you'd want to know. Of course, the Yankees were looking for a home run hitter, and I knew I wasn't hitting home runs in the minors. I always had a good batting average.

In fact, talking to Lou Gehrig in the evening at one of the events we attended here in New York City—both Lou and I came from New York City so we would run into each other once in a while—he said, "They're talking about you taking my job."

I laughed. I said, "Hey, don't worry about that. The way you play I'll never take your job. All I want to do is get to the major leagues."

In talking to Paul Krichell, I said, "I think I can play in the major leagues and if you can make a deal for me, fine." A lot of people forget I had broken my leg in Columbus the year before—in 1935—even though I hit about .335 or something. I was hitting about .350 when I broke it. I guess they figured there was some damaged goods there, but the Brooklyn club made me go through some doctors to make sure that the leg was all right.

The Yankees didn't need anybody. New York still had George McQuinn, you know. He was in the organization at the same time, so I had two pretty good first basemen ahead of me.

They made a deal. They got Johnny McCarthy and Buzz Boyle, who they traded for Jimmy Gleeson. That was one of George Weiss's big deals. He got, I think, $60,000 for McCarthy from the Giants and then he got another 75 or so for Gleeson, who he got for Boyle, so he ended up with a 100-and-something thousand, which at that time was a lot of money.

That was one of his big deals. In fact, I think that was one of the *big* things that he got his reputation on—being a smart operator.

BK: Brooklyn later traded you to Boston.

BH: They brought [Dolph] Camilli in there to hit home runs. Larry MacPhail wanted a home run hitter.

It's funny you brought that up because I got to looking at my record myself and I said, "Geez, I only played 71 games [in the field] in my third year after hitting .300 two years in a row."

BK: You pinch-hit a lot that year.

BH: Yeah, I did. I think at one time I got 9 out of 10 before he [manager Burleigh Grimes] put me in the ball game.

Grimes and I had our problems. Mr. Grimes did not like Mr. Stengel and he knew Mr. Stengel and I were friends, so it didn't work out.

BK: You played for Stengel twice.

BH: Yes. Casey was one of the nicest people and he was a good baseball man. He was not the clown that people thought he was.

In the winter of '35 the trade was made for me to go to Brooklyn and I think they [Brooklyn] traded Sam Leslie back to the Giants. I was hitting about .320, and I ran into a real bad period right toward the end of the season. I went about 0 for 20 or 25. It happens.

We're on the tail-end of the season and I guess we only had a couple more games to play and Waite Hoyt and I went in the hotel—the Edgewater Beach—in Chicago and had a beer just before the midnight curfew. We had our beers up at the bar and Casey and his wife were sitting at a table. We finished our beers just about five minutes to twelve and we got up to leave. We were heading out and Casey yelled, "Hey, Bud! Come here!" He let Waite go on his business.

I went over and he said, "Sit down." So I sat down with Mr. and Mrs. Stengel. He called the waiter over and he said, "What are you drinking?" I said, "Beer."

He said, "Listen, I owe you something. You may not know this, but nobody in the Brooklyn organization ever saw you play in Columbus in 1935." I was on option from the Yankees to the Columbus club, which was part of the Cardinal organization. He said, "Nobody in our organization saw you play but I called up all my friends in the American Association and they said to sign you. You made the deal stand up. I owe you a beer." (Laughs) He was that type of fellow.

BK: When you were with Boston in 1940—the year you had the 10 consecutive hits—you had a terrible season for you. What happened?

BH: I'd have 4 hits and then nothing. That was the year I hit .234.

In fact, Jo Jo Moore, who was then playing center field for the Giants, was having the same type of year. You'd get 4 hits and then you'd go 0 for 4 for the next 4 days and then you'd have 4 more hits. We just couldn't put anything together and we used to commiserate with each other. (Laughs) It helped just to talk with him to know somebody else was in the same boat as you. Misery loves company. (Laughs)

BK: You came back well.

BH: I figured it was one of those years and I guess you're entitled to one out of four. The other thing was, we figured if you have two or three good years in the major leagues they'd keep you up there for another couple of years. Then the war interfered and there was nothing I could do about that.

Ed Barrow said to me when I had to go in the service, "I thought we had a first baseman for a couple of more years."

BK: Were you drafted?

BH: Oh, yeah, but I'd beaten them to the punch—I signed up in the Navy where I got a commission. I figured I didn't go to college for nothing.

I used to play against Birdie Tebbetts [in college] when he was up in Providence and I was at Manhattan. We used to battle each other every year. When it was about time for me to go in the service, I got a letter from Birdie and he was already in the service. He told me, "If you have to go in the Army, let me know—I have a spot for you." I thought that was very nice, very thoughtful.

But I went in the Navy. I figured if I had to go, I wanted to be clean and neat and not into the mud. (Laughs)

BK: You played in the World Series just before you left.

BH: Yeah, in '42. It was pretty exciting until I busted my thumb in the third game trying to bunt. And I could bunt fairly well. (Laughs)

Joe McCarthy [Yankee manager] never bunted in the first inning in his life, that I knew of. I had been hitting eighth down in St. Louis for two games and I ended up 3 for 8 and now we came up [to New York] and he moves me up to second, behind [Phil] Rizzuto.

Rizzuto gets on base. Ernie White is pitching and he's [McCarthy] got me bunting. It's a game of inches—the difference between where I had the tip of my thumb and the bat was maybe a half-inch but the ball just caught it and busted the top of that thumb right off. It was my throwing hand, so that put me right out of the Series. It was only a little tip but I couldn't throw. If it had been on the other hand, I'd have been able to play. They had to bring Gerry Priddy in to play first base from then on. We lost that game and the next two and the Series.

BK: Who was the best player you saw?

BH: Best player I saw? I gotta categorize it. The best player I ever saw was Babe Ruth. The reason I say that, I put it in three different categories: home run hitters, outfielders, and pitching. He could do it all. Nobody else could. Some could do the hitting, some could do the throwing. Babe could do the throwing from the outfield and all the rest.

But the best hitter I ever saw was [Ted] Williams and the best ballplayer, other than pitching, was [Joe] DiMaggio, by far. He was just something else—great to watch, great to play with. Poetry in motion. He never looked like he was trying. He was always there. When the ball was hit, he had those long strides and, shoot, he'd be there before you'd know it and make the plays.

BK: Babe Ruth coached for the Dodgers in the 1938 when you were there.

BH: He was just a fine human being. Naturally he didn't have the greatest education in the world, but I thought he handled himself very well, as far as the public went, and I thought he was a great advantage to the game. I thought he gave the game something that nobody else ever gave it. Actually, he gave it the impetus after the 1919 World Series problem. He saved the game.

You know, a lot of people want to beat him down, but he never hurt anybody. He was always trying to help people, and I never heard him say anything against anybody the year I was with him. I spent time with him in his home and at the ballpark.

To me, he was the greatest ballplayer that every lived for these reasons: he could pitch, he could play the outfield, he could play first base, and he could hit, he could throw, and he could run. What else do you want? Most people can just do one thing or two things.

What Larry MacPhail wanted him to do [with Brooklyn in 1938] was hit home runs in exhibition games. He wasn't looking for him to do anything more than that. Larry MacPhail was looking for somebody who could put people in the stands, to play exhibition games. That's all. And he did it well and he accepted it in a very gracious manner. He knew what his position was and he was a very fine gentleman with it.

A lot of people don't understand. He not only saved the game but, to me, he was the greatest ballplayer that ever lived because he could do so many other things. [Henry] Aaron hit home runs and [Lou] Gehrig hit home runs, but can either one of 'em pitch? Go ahead and look at it. As far as a baseball player went, he was the best that ever lived and that goes for Ted Williams, DiMaggio—just look at it all. He stole home ten times. He was pretty sharp, too. He knew when we were gonna steal.

I enjoyed him and he was a human being. He didn't try to put on airs. He was just Babe Ruth all his life. He didn't try to be somebody else. I'm not gonna moralize; I'm talking about a baseball player.

I'll tell you a true story. I'm a Catholic and at the time he was with us in '38, we had to eat fish on Friday. We pulled into Buffalo to play an exhibition game in 1938. He got off the train—he was the first one off—and got a cab and went to, I think, the Lexington Hotel in Buffalo. We dressed in the hotel for the exhibition game. I came in the hotel maybe a half-hour later and I was paged to come up and have breakfast with him, up in his room.

I went up, naturally, because I thought he was great. It was nice to be around him. It was a Friday morning. He said, "I want you to have breakfast with me." I said, "Fine, Babe, but . . ." He said, "'But'? Leave 'but' to me, please." And he went to another room and ordered breakfast.

I had a lobster à la Newburg omelet! I'd never had it before! (Laughs) He said, "I know you're a Catholic. I know that you can't eat meat today." That will give you an idea how he could think. I've never had a breakfast like it before or since. (Laughs)

I don't care what all these people write and they make movie pictures and everything else. To me, he was one of the finest men I ever met.

BK: Who was the toughest pitcher on you?

BH: I always laugh at that because they were all tough. There was nothing easy. Actually the toughest pitcher I ever saw—and I only saw him in spring training—to see the ball and catch it on the way was Red Ruffing. I only played against him in spring training.

I hit against the best they had in the National League—Dizzy Dean and [Carl] Hubbell and you name 'em—but for a ball that would catch up to me so quickly before I was ready, he had a delivery that looked like a very easy motion and all of a sudden the ball was upon you. I thought to myself, "Geez, this would be tough to hit against if I had to do this every time." But I suppose if you saw him a couple of more times you'd sort of pick up on it and be able to catch his wind-up and look for where his release came from.

When he got quite sick I decided to write him a letter. I was working out with the Yankees when I was at Manhattan College and the Yankees were playing the Athletics. Lefty Grove was pitching for the Athletics and I don't know who was pitching for the Yankees, but it was a nothing-to-nothing ball game going into the bottom of the ninth inning. The Yankees got a man on second base and McCarthy sent Ruff up to hit and, boy, he hit the first pitch—almost took Grove's ear off—into center field with the base hit that won the ball game.

So I wrote him when he was sick, "One of the great things that I ever remembered about you, I know you could hit the ball." He was quite sick at the time—in a wheelchair—and I was hoping it might sort of build his spirits a little bit.

BK: Do you get fan mail?

BH: A little here and a little there, but not enough to worry about. I understand business and I understand baseball, and baseball is business, and it's like everything else. It's the kids who know the ballplayers and that will control who's gonna get the letters. I understand that. It doesn't bother me at all.

Lefty Gomez—now there was a great pitcher and a lot of people don't remember. Kids today, they don't remember him that much and they should. Life goes on, though, and the kids today know the players of today.

BK: It seems a shame that players like you who gave so much to the game aren't remembered better today.

BH: I'd like to get somebody to recognize the fellows like us, at my age, who are not in the pension plan. The *only* major sport which did not take care of the players before the pension plan started is baseball. A lot of people know it, but nobody does anything about it. Apparently nobody wants to even get involved with it.

BK: What about the work Early Wynn has done?

BH: You know what he did? He took care of the people who were in the original pension, that's all. He did get them their money. He only took care of the one he was in—the original pension.

Eddie Lopat lived right down the street from me, so I got the news on this, too. He was in on the original pension—it's gonna be doubled for them. But the people before that—nothing.

Football took care of theirs, basketball took care of theirs. I have a brother played five years professional basketball, he's getting $500 a month and they're gonna double that. They're taking care of those who weren't in on the original pension.

I belong to two organizations in baseball. I write to them and they're all millionaires now, so all that I get back is, "We can't do much about that."

It soured me on baseball pretty much. I can live without it, but I'm still working at 80 to just keep the house I'm living in. I've been in the trucking business—the sales end of it—since 1947. I'm still able to make a buck, not a lot of money but enough to keep the house. I lost my wife, so I'm living here by myself and I try to keep things going.

The reason I've soured on it is the way this thing's been handled. A hundred or two hundred a month isn't gonna help me; I'll be able to manage until they put the lid on my face, which could happen any time. (Laughs)

BK: There are guys a hundred dollars a month would mean a lot to.

BH: My argument is, rather than look for a handout, they could have a little pride that's coming to them and use it the way they see fit and not have somebody say, "Oh, you need this? Let's see if I can get it for you."

The other thing is, a lot of fellows lost out during the war. I was out of the majors in May of '46, Marius Russo was out in August of '46. It started the first day of '47. What are you gonna do with these people—throw 'em out? That's exactly what happened.

I wish there were some newspapermen I could talk to, but the ones I knew are either dead or retired.

BK: Would you go back 60 years and be a ballplayer again?

BH: Sure. I love the game. When you first start it's "Geez, boy, I'm getting paid for something I really love to do."

John Aloysius (Buddy) Hassett

Born September 5, 1911, New York, NY
Ht. 5′11″ Wt. 180 Batted and Threw Left

Year	Team	G	AB	R	H	2B	3B	HR	RBI	SB	BA	SA
1936	BrkN	156*	635	79	197	29	11	3	82	5	.310	.405
1937		137	556	71	169	31	6	1	53	13	.304	.387
1938		115	335	49	98	11	6	0	40	3	.293	.361
1939	BosN	147	590	72	182	15	3	2	60	13	.308	.354
1940		124	458	59	107	19	4	0	27	4	.234	.293
1941		118	405	59	120	9	4	1	33	10	.296	.346
1942	NYA	132	538	80	153	16	6	5	48	5	.284	.364
7 years		929	3517	469	1026	130	40	12	343	53	.292	.362

**Led League*

World Series

Year	Team	G	AB	R	H	2B	3B	HR	RBI	SB	BA	SA
1942	NYA	3	9	1	3	1	0	0	2	0	.333	.444

Strikeout totals by year: 1936–17, 1937–19, 1938–19, 1939–14, 1940–16, 1941–15, 1942–16; 7-year total–116.

TOT PRESSNELL

Milwaukee Mainstay

1938–1942

Sixty years ago farm systems were just beginning and most minor league clubs were still independently owned, and those clubs owned their own players. This was one way minor league teams supported themselves. They would sell their players who were successful to a team in a higher classification.

***Above:* Tot Pressnell (George Brace photo).**

But if the team did not need money or a player was an integral part of that club's success, he would not be sold. The classic example of this is Lefty Grove, whom Baltimore refused to sell until the offer got so high it could no longer be refused. As a consequence, Grove toiled for the Orioles for five years (gaining 108 wins) before getting to the majors.

Grove is just one example. There were many others who performed so well for their minor league clubs that their major league debut was delayed well beyond the point of reason. A few examples are Freddie Fitzsimmons (four years at Indianapolis), Remy Kremer (seven years with Oakland), Jimmy Ripple (six years in Montreal), and Tot Pressnell.

Tot Pressnell was a *good* minor league pitcher. In eight seasons, he won 107 games. In 1932, at Longview in the Texas League, he won 16 games and the Milwaukee Brewers of the American Association bought his contract. He would be employed there through 1937, during which time he would compile a 71-56 (.559) record for a team which was barely over .500 for those five years.

But Tot had a handicap. He was older than the average promising minor leaguer, which limited the interest of the major league clubs. Feelers were put out and one legitimate offer was made, but Milwaukee, the team and the city, liked him so there he stayed.

The reason he was older is simple—he began his career later than most players. In 1930, when he signed with Topeka of the Western League, he gave his birth year as 1907, but it was actually 1906. Then, as now, teams are reluctant to bring someone with a few years on him up to the majors.

In 1937, however, the Boston Braves, a team which could rightly be called the Browns of the National League, gambled on two older veteran minor league pitchers, Jim Turner and Lou Fette. Turner, 31, had played minor league ball for 12 years, and Fette, 30, had been around for nine. Both won 20 games as rookies and a few clubs took notice.

The Brooklyn Dodgers were going nowhere in those days. They had not been in the first division since 1932, so they took a chance on a pair of older minor league veterans: Luke Hamlin (eight years in the minors coupled with one lackluster season with Detroit five years earlier) and Tot Pressnell. And again the veteran pitchers came through. The two old guys ended up leading the seventh-place Dodgers in wins.

Two years earlier Hamlin and Pressnell had each won 19 games to lead the Brewers to the apex of minor league baseball: the American Association championship, victory in the first-ever Shaughnessy playoffs, and a five-game trouncing of International League champ Buffalo in the Junior World Series.

Tot Pressnell made the most of his belated rise to the big leagues. He was nearly 32 when he got there, but even with the late start, he put in five seasons in the big time.

* * *

BK: How did you get your nickname?

TOT PRESSNELL: That's been asked to me by hundreds of people in their letters, how I got the name of Tot. The only way I know—and remember, I've had it ever since I was a little kid—I came from a big family of eight children and I was the baby. I can just hear my mother say, "Pick up that little tot and let's get goin'," or something like that. It's been with me all my life and I'm known better by Tot. Very few people know me as Forest.

BK: You didn't begin playing professionally until you were nearly 24 years old.

TP: I lied about my age on the first contract I wrote, so it wouldn't look so bad. I was born in 1906 instead of 1907. There wasn't any better minor league ballplayer than I was. Pitcher. My record will prove that I was the best pitcher in Triple-A ball. I never got a chance to go [to the majors] until I was 32 for the reason that Milwaukee was locally owned. They weren't owned by a big league ballclub. They wouldn't let me go. I can show you clippings in papers where in 1934 the Pittsburgh Pirates offered $25,000 for me and they wouldn't let me go because they'd just have to replace me with somebody else. Back in the 1930s, $25,000 was the equivalent of a half a million dollars today.

I was in high school till I was 21. I failed two or three years and I just didn't wanna quit. I just kept goin'. A gentleman here in town by the name of Del Drake—played with Detroit in 1911—and he got me a contract. That's the way I got started in the Western League in Topeka.

Back then they didn't want to take you up to the major leagues after you were 30. Jim Turner and Lou Fette were two of the greatest ones to come out of Triple-A ball and they went to Boston in 1937 and they both won 20 ballgames. That kinda opened up the age limit. It made me look a little better.

BK: Were you frustrated by not being sold to the majors earlier?

TP: It didn't bother me. I don't know why, but I loved Milwaukee. That ballclub we had in 1936 in Milwaukee, where we won the pennant and the playoffs and the Little World Series, that ballclub would finish 1, 2, 3 in the majors today. No doubt about it.

I loved Milwaukee. I think I could have become mayor of Milwaukee if I'd have stayed there a couple more years. The fans really loved me. In 1937, they had a day for me. Gave me a car.

BK: Do you remember your first start for Brooklyn?

TP: You bet I do! I pitched a shutout against Philadelphia [a final 9–0 win]. At the time it didn't worry me too much, but I pitched that shutout in the smallest ballpark in the major leagues—Baker Bowl. I just didn't think about it until I went back the next time and seen how short those fences were. It scared you. Luckily we never returned there to play. We changed over to the old Athletic park.

BK: That first year with Brooklyn, they moved you from starting to the bullpen.

TP: We were a bottom-place ballclub that year. I got along real well up to about July. I was the leading pitcher on the ballclub—I had 11 wins and 9 losses. I think they played a dirty trick in order to get me to get on the losing side, so the money wouldn't have to come in next year.

We went into Boston and I was used to beating Boston or they would beat me 1 to nothing. We were to play a doubleheader. I was to start the second ball game and I was sittin' in the dugout. Burleigh Grimes was the manager; our pitcher got in trouble in the seventh inning and he said, "Go to the bullpen, Tot." Why, I pert near fell over! I never heard of a man relieving in the first game that was gonna start the second game. I went in and got credit for the loss.

I went in the clubhouse to change clothes [between games] and he come over and he threw me the warm-up ball and said, "Here, take this. See if you can lose this game." Boy, that rubbed me the wrong way. I went to Babe Phelps, my catcher, and I told Babe, "Don't give me any signs. I'm just goin' out there and I'm gonna show that guy how to lose a ballgame." And I did. I didn't get anybody out in the first inning.

That was the one of the rottenest deals I ever had. That made me 11 and 11. Matter of fact, I can show you clippings in the paper where the reporters even said I got an awful bad deal in Boston.

BK: How was Grimes as a manager?

TP: Terrible. I just couldn't get along with him at all and I think that set the whole thing off. He fought with everybody.

BK: After Grimes, Leo Durocher took over as manager.

TP: Leo was great! I mean, Leo was as good a manager as you'd want. He'd give you the devil once in a while, but if you'd get in trouble for knockin' some guy down up there at the home plate he'd come out and protect you. He was a great little shortstop. He was well-liked by all the boys that I know of.

BK: You had excellent control.

Tot Pressnell (courtesy National Pastime).

TP: I had the best control. Jimmie Wilson, when I went to Chicago, he told me, "Tot," he said, "one of your troubles is your strike zone is *too* good." I walked *very* few men [2.3 per nine innings]. I'd get the ball over, I know that.

I think what got me in trouble was my knuckleball. I was a knuckleball pitcher. I always tried to get ahead of 'em before I showed 'em the knuckleball and probably the knuckleball was when I would walk men. A lot of times I'd walk 'em on purpose, like Johnny Mize—I never gave him anything but a knuckleball. He was great.

BK: Where did you learn the knuckleball?

TP: I really don't know. When I was in high school I played left field. I don't remember where or when I ever turned over to pitchin'.

BK: Babe Ruth was a Dodgers coach when you were with them.

TP: I knew him very well. I was with him all summer. About anything you say about Babe Ruth is true. He was a lone wolf, I would say, but a very nice man. He was a gentleman but everybody knows that his morals were terrible and he drank a lot, which you couldn't stop him. A guy performs and hits all the home runs, you can't stop him. He was just hired as a coach and a drawing card. He played exhibition games. He played first base when we played exhibition games.

Babe Ruth was never able to take signs when he was up to bat. He hit whenever he wanted to. Every man on the team is up there not on his own; whatever the coach wants him to do, he'll do. But Babe wasn't that way. He had no signs—he hit when he wanted to. He could hit 3 and nothin' or any time he wanted to hit, he'd hit.

He was a great outfielder. They claimed that he never made a bad throw to the wrong base. He had a spot in the Yankee Stadium about halfway between first and home where the ball hit so regular that it had the grass tore up—where he was throwin' balls into home plate. His legs were little but from his waist up he was a big man. He was great.

BK: After the 1940 season, you were sold three times before the '41 season began.

TP: Oh yeah! In the first place I went to the Cardinals and Cincinnati wanted me so the Cardinals shipped me over to Cincinnati. Jimmie Wilson was there at the time as a coach for Bill McKechnie. Jimmie was gonna be made manager of the Chicago Cubs and Jim liked me. Always did like me, so he bought me from Cincinnati. That's how I got switched around for all four clubs. I never reported to any of 'em except Chicago. I knew I was about through at that time. I came out with a winning record.

BK: What did you do when you left baseball after the 1942 season?

TP: I went right to work for the Marathon Oil Company—23 years.

BK: Is there one game that stands out?

TP: I think a couple of 'em. One was against Boston one day. I had a no-hitter up to the eighth inning and the worst hitter on the team broke it up on me, and it ended up a two-hit ball game and I won it, 1 to nothing. The little shortstop, Rabbit Warstler, got the first hit. And Buddy Hassett, he come along and got the other.

Buddy was my roommate in Brooklyn. He was a peach of a roommate. Nothin' crooked about that guy! I roomed with KiKi Cuyler at times. Great fella. In Chicago, I roomed with Cuyler again and Claude Passeau was my roomie. I roomed with Waite Hoyt, too, my first year in Brooklyn. He was a great fella, too.

And the other one was the Johnny Vander Meer second consecutive no-hitter. I pitched in that game. Ival Goodman hit me on the kneecap with a line drive and that was the end of me. I was in the hospital when the game was over. Max Butcher started the ball game and I think they got four runs off of him in the third inning and I went in and I pitched three-and-two-thirds innings. I think they got one run off of me and then I got hit.

BK: Who was the best player you saw?

TP: The best pitcher I think I would say was Carl Hubbell. He'd be my choice for a lefthanded pitcher. And there was some other great pitchers in the league: Mort Cooper, Claude Passeau, Max Lanier, Van Mungo—he was good but he just didn't keep in training, ol' Fat Freddie Fitzsimmons, Charlie Root. The best hitter—I had the most trouble with Johnny Mize.

BK: How does baseball today compare to baseball 50 or 60 years ago?

TP: I'll tell you what I think of today—it's boring to watch. And I would say there's 350 ballplayers in the major leagues today that couldn't have played Triple-A ball back in the '30s and '40s.

My lawyer and I went up to Detroit to see a ballgame. The Yankees were playin'. We left in the fourth inning and they had played two hours then. We drove clear back home and looked in the paper. They played four hours and ten minutes in a nine-inning ballgame! I don't know how they [the fans] stay there that long. I don't even like to watch it on television that long.

BK: Do you receive many autograph requests?

TP: I get 'em all the time. I'm in the Ohio Hall of Fame and I get pictures. If they just send a little card I don't like that; I send 'em a picture and autograph it.

I get lots and lots—hundreds—of letters. I've even got letters from Sydney, Australia, for autographs. And from Canada. I think I get so many because they know that I'm alive.

I had so many things. My lawyer and I, we shipped 'em up to New York. They're gonna be on auction. Baseballs autographed by Babe and Honus Wagner, Babe Ruth's glove, and about eight bats with '38 and '39 World Series and All-Star lineups on 'em. And a hundred pictures—all of 'em autographed—I had in my den. I sent them along.

I was just leery about whether I'd be treated right with 'em. I've been cheated out of so much stuff by men up in New York, it's unbelievable. You've gotta be careful. I've got movies I took back when I was in Brooklyn. My wife took 'em in 1938. I made tapes of 'em and I shipped one to New

York and they said, "If we use it on HBO we'll send you a thousand dollars." They took it and they made a copy and that's the last I heard of it. I had Babe Ruth and Lou Gehrig and Lefty Gomez and all the great ones down in spring training, and then we ended up in Ebbets Field.

BK: Any regrets?

TP: Not a bit. I go over 'em every night. I've got a nice fireplace and I sit here and if I'm alone I can go back and I can name every guy on my first ballclub. I've got five grandchildren and four great-grandchildren and I run movies of baseball for 'em and I'll name 'em off as they come along and they can't get over how my memory is that good to name these guys back 50 years ago. I thank the good Lord every night that my memory is still very good.

One of my good friends just died, Augie Galan. Augie was center fielder for the Cubs when I was up there. Great ballplayer. Great kid. I thank the good Lord every day for another day.

BK: Would you be a ballplayer again?

TP: Not in the condition it's in today. Money has ruined it. We played because we loved our sport. We made good money for the '30s. It was the worst [time]. I made $8,000; that was the most I ever made, but I lived like a king. I had a new automobile every year, nice home, lived in the best hotels, travelled by pullman train. I told different people that I had just as much as these guys do today except a lot of money in the bank. I don't believe I'd want to go back in it today.

Forest Charles (Tot) Pressnell

Born August 8, 1906, Findlay, OH
Ht. 5′10½″ Wt. 175 Batted and Threw Right

Year	Team	G	IP	W	L	PCT	BB	SO	H	SHO	SV	ERA
1938	BrkN	43	192	11	14	.440	56	57	209	1	3	3.56
1939		31	156.2	9	7	.563	33	43	171	2	2	4.02
1940		24	68.1	6	5	.545	17	21	58	1	2	3.69
1941	ChiN	29	70	5	3	.625	23	27	69	0	1	3.09
1942		27	39.1	1	1	.500	5	9	40	0	4	5.49
5 years		154	526.1	32	30	.516	134	157	547	4	12	3.80

BIBLIOGRAPHY

Bak, Richard. *Cobb Would Have Caught It.* Detroit: Great Lakes Books, 1991.

Carter, Craig, ed. *The Complete Baseball Record Book—1990.* St. Louis: *The Sporting News,* 1990.

Charlton, James, ed. *The Baseball Chronology.* New York: Macmillan, 1991.

Greenberg, Hank; Ira Berkow, ed. *The Story of My Life.* New York: Times Books, 1989.

Neft, David S., and Richard M. Cohen. *The Sports Encyclopedia: Baseball.* 10th ed. New York: St. Martin's, 1990.

Reichler, Joseph L.; revised by Ken Samelson. *The Baseball Record Companion.* New York: Macmillan, 1993.

Shatzkin, Mike, ed. *The Ballplayers.* New York: William Morrow, 1990.

Thorn, John, et al., eds. *Total Baseball.* 2nd ed. New York: Warner, 1991.

Wolff, Rick, editorial director. *The Baseball Encyclopedia.* 9th ed. New York: Macmillan, 1993.

Various editions of the following were referred to:

Baseball Register, published annually by *The Sporting News.*

Who's Who in Baseball, published annually by Baseball Magazine Co., New York.

INDEX

Numbers in **boldface** *refer to pages with photos.*